Life After Suicide

The Impact of Suicide on the Ones Left Behind

W. Brandon Callor

DEDICATION

I dedicate this book to all the families who are challenged with the loss of someone dear to them due to suicide. I especially want to dedicate this book to my mother-in-law, who has taught me how to persevere by faith, hope, and charity, and also to my father-in-law for his example of strength through troubled times. Finally, I dedicate this book to my wife, who suffered alongside me as difficult memories were brought to the surface with each and every chapter we toiled over in order to bring this story to light.

TABLE OF CONTENTS

ACKNOWLEDGMENTS

I would like to acknowledge the remarkable efforts of the research team from the University of Utah. You are wonderful and fantastic teammates who are making a difference. To Doug and Hilary, I'd like to thank you for what you have taught me and have allowed me to do in regards to suicide research. Todd, I am inspired by the work that you have done as chief medical examiner and am greatly indebted for your belief in my work. You are a wonderful mentor. I would also like to acknowledge all my fantastic employees and friends, who have stood by me and buoyed me up during tumultuous times in my life. Most importantly, I'd like to thank my family for their love and support. Without you I wouldn't be here. I love you all.

Disclaimer and Introduction

This book is meant to be a companion and a guide through your grieving process. The purpose of this book is to share my journey of healing from the perspective of one who examines the dead for a living and has spoken to thousands of people just like you. It is not intended to replace professional counselling.

I expect two things from you as you read my book. First, read with an open mind. Second, choose one of the seven techniques discussed in Chapters 4 through 21, and practice it for at least one month. I warn you, however, if you are tender or in any way fragile right now, do not continue reading. Seek professional counseling and allow yourself a few months to grieve before you read any further. Throughout this book I will talk about the process involved in performing autopsies as well as other practices involved with being a medical examiner assistant. My writing is candid and your heart and mind need to be in a safe place before you continue. When you are ready, please continue.

As an employee of the Utah Department of Health, it is my responsibility to inform my readers that the opinions shared in this book are my own and do not reflect that of the State of Utah. It is my intention to provide information that both educates and promotes well-being.

As a program manager for the State of Utah, my responsibilities cover a unique area. It's important that you understand my distinct perspective in order to fully appreciate the story I'm about to tell you. For fifteen years, I've assisted the forensic pathologists with performing autopsies at the Office of the Medical Examiner. Those of us involved with the process feel a special connection to the work; others on the outside think it's morbid. In any case, I've always found it to be interesting and intriguing.

I have been drawn to mysteries my whole life. Who doesn't like a good puzzle, right? The feeling of accomplishment you get from completing a puzzle or solving a mystery is very satisfying. I feel lucky that I get to be part of solving mysteries every day. Unfortunately, many of them are very sad and some are bizarre.

I find death to be one of life's greatest mysteries. It is a respecter of no person regardless of influence or power.

It will claim each of us someday. Most likely it will be sudden and unexpected. That's when my office gets involved. One of the responsibilities of the medical examiner is to diagnose the cause and manner of death on sudden and unexpected deaths.

Death doesn't take a holiday, so naturally, neither do we. We deal with death on a daily basis. It's like getting a daily dose of perspective. I've helped examine friends and neighbors, and although their deaths were very sad, I've always found something to appreciate. I've been able to find comfort through understanding the pathophysiology of the disease process. Some diseases take a while to claim their victim, which gives the patient and their family time to prepare. Often, but not always, this affords them time to cope and come to terms with their eventual demise. My brother-in-law's suicide death in Autumn 2014 was different. It was senseless and sudden.

Chapter 1
Time Matters

People will apologize as if they had anything to do with your tragedy. Some will say, "I know how you feel," as if that's supposed to help. I learned a long time ago that people don't know what to say or how to react to death.

Honestly, what do you say to somebody who has just lost everything? I don't know, but I decided years ago that when it happened to me I would cut them some slack and forgive them before they even uttered a word. I told myself that whatever came out of their mouth was simply an expression of their love.

Let's be honest, I don't know you and I can't even begin to know how *you* feel. I only know how I feel and I know that the suicide of my loved one turned my life upside down. If it compares in any way to how you feel, then I believe the principles in this book will help you recover from your pain and anguish. I learned these principles firsthand, not only from the work I do every day as a medical examiner assistant, but out of necessity as I began digging myself out of a pit of despair. By implementing the strategies discussed in the following chapters, I learned how to cope with the suicide of my brother-in-law, David.

My family's tragic story began just before six o'clock on a cold October morning, a fact I was unaware of for almost two hours. It was my day to take lead in assisting the medical examiner with autopsy service, so I arrived fifteen minutes before seven in the morning. My task for the day would be to eviscerate, which included the traditional Y-shaped incision using a scalpel in a surgical-type fashion. To give you an idea of the process, the initial cut begins at the front of each shoulder and meets at the sternum, creating a V-shape. The next cut begins at the bottom of the V and runs directly down past the navel and stops just above the pubic bone. The skin is surgically reflected back to create an opening and then the rib cage is cut away to reveal the heart and lungs. After the body cavity is entirely open, each of the organs is removed by the assistant and examined by the forensic pathologist.

When I arrived that morning, the building was cold and quiet as usual. The night shift morgue clerk was still in her call room, so I was alone in the reception area. There were only a few yellow case folders on the desk in front of me. Each case folder represented a person who had died throughout the night and was brought to the medical examiner's office for examination. We have an explicit obligation, mandated by state law, of determining the cause and manner of death of each individual within our jurisdiction.

I read the investigative reports that lay on top of each of the case files on the reception desk. According to the reports we were investigating a possible accidental overdose and two presumed self-inflicted gunshot wounds. This meant that I needed to set up paperwork and test tubes and perform x-rays prior to the doctor arriving.

At this point the only unusual thing about the day was that there were so few individuals to be examined. Generally, we examine between 8 and 10 people each day, so to have only three was not typical. This meant that I would have time later in the day to work on administrative tasks.

We were so short staffed that it required me to be in autopsy more than 80% of my time. That didn't leave much time for managing a morgue with all of its complexities. It would be a good day for me to catch up on recruitment, purchasing, employee performance evaluations, and facility management. You name it, and it was going to get done.

I scanned my ID badge to the walk-in cooler and waited for the large, stainless steel door to slide open. I entered the frigid 38 degree room and located my first patient, who had an alleged self-inflicted gunshot wound. I grabbed the edge of the stainless steel autopsy cart and dragged it out of the cooler. The carts were nearly 200 pounds of pure stainless steel with casters the size of salad plates. Adding 200 pounds of human remains made it difficult to maneuver, but fifteen years of doing it had trained my muscles to maneuver the corners respectfully without banging into the walls.

The cart trailed down the hall as I walked backwards, dragging it with me to the x-ray room. The x-ray room was small and warm. It had barely enough room for the x-ray equipment and the autopsy cart. I situated the x-ray machine over the table and placed a digital x-ray plate under the patient's head. Then I walked around the corner behind a lead-lined wall to the control panel and zapped the x-ray.

I performed the same routine for the second self-inflicted gunshot wound victim. At this point, I was oblivious to the fact that there were 11 more people elsewhere in the state of Utah who were found dead that morning but had yet to be received by the medical examiner. If I had opened the database I might have discovered that fact, but for some reason, I didn't. Little did I know, one of those eleven was my brother-in-law.

I finished downloading the x-ray images to the computer system and pushed the autopsy cart back into the cooler. The paperwork was all set up, and the rest of my staff had arrived by this time and was bustling about helping to set up instruments and test tubes.

As my staff continued to prepare for the day, I informed them that I was going upstairs to my office to get some admin work done prior to autopsy. At this point, we still had about thirty minutes to an hour before the doctors would arrive, at which time we would get started with exams.

I walked up the dimly lit, dusty, steep staircase in the back hallway. I've always thought of those stairs as a secret entrance to someplace spooky. They were never used by the public and rarely used by the staff. They lead directly to the chief medical examiner's office and a small conference room at the end of a long hallway.

My office was directly behind the chief medical examiner's office. In fact, it was meant to serve as a library and storage closet. It was a long, thin room that ran behind all four medical examiner's private offices. The only way to get to it was through a door behind each of their desks.

It was awkward for me to excuse myself through their office when I wanted to get to my desk, so I preferred to get as much as possible done early so I could avoid the uneasiness of intruding. Most of the time I would check the attendance board and find a doctor who was out for the day and just use their office to enter and exit mine. On a day when all four were in, though, it was tricky.

This early in the morning I didn't need to worry about intruding. The upstairs floor was eerily empty and dark. The only light came from a parking lot lamp that peaked through the windows running the length of the hall.

Office staff wouldn't arrive until eight o'clock, so nobody was there to turn on the lights.

Fortunately, I'd been doing this for a long time, so I'd grown accustomed to dark and spooky. I actually preferred the dark, so I made my way through the shadows until I reached my desk.

I flipped the switch to overhead fluorescent lights and the mood changed instantly. Warm yellow lights flickered at first, and then sustained with a faint hum that my ears eventually dismissed. I thought this was going to be a great day. I hadn't had one in a very long time and I was looking forward to it.

Soon, I was on a roll typing recruitment memos and purchase order requests. I wasn't paying attention to anything else, including the time. I didn't even notice that I had missed a few calls on my cell phone from my wife until one of my employees entered my office and told me that she had been trying to reach me.

Apparently my wife called directly into the morgue to get a hold of me after I didn't answer my cell phone. According to my employee her call was accidently dropped when he tried to forward it. He sensed the urgency in her voice, so he ran up the stairs to inform me rather than waiting for her to call back.

The look on his face when he told me to call my wife instilled horror in my mind. I immediately began to worry about my children. My heart told me that something terrible had happened.

As I began dialing her on my phone another employee rushed into the room and said, "Just go home. We'll cover your shift today. Just go!" Apparently my wife did call back and this employee sensed the same urgency.

At that point I knew bad news was coming and my heart sank. My mind was conflicted between wanting to know but not wanting to hear the bad news.

My wife answered the phone and said, "Brand, it's David. He's coming to your office."

The world suddenly shifted and it actually felt like it started spinning backwards. Although her message was clear, I didn't understand what she was trying to tell me. Whether it was her panicked tone or the unbelievable message, my brain was overwhelmed and scrambled in time.

The two sweet men who ran to warn me now stood motionless, staring at me with suspense in their eyes. I stared back holding the phone to my ear and stood like stone for what felt like a lifetime. As I listened to my wife's trembling voice on the other end of the line, my mind wandered. I began thinking about David's birthday parties, lizard hunting expeditions, backyard campouts, Scouting expos, and video game battles. I remembered all the times in the past my wife would call and ask me to meet David next door at Primary Children's Hospital because he had gone into ketoacidosis. I recollected rushing away from work to meet David at his bedside. My face became numb and tears welled up in my eyes. I would have given anything for this to be one of those calls.

That fateful October morning has played out in my mind like a bad rerun. You know the one. It seems to always be running whenever you turn on the television. The image is so familiar it's practically burned into the screen. It mocks you as if to say, "Here I am again, whether you like it or not." Well, this moment in my life is always running in the back of my mind and will forever be burned into my soul whether I like it or not. I thought I could handle just about anything the world had to throw at me, until then. David's death caused me to reexamine my life.

Until that time, days of the week meant nothing to me. My office was open 24/7. One day in my world was no different from any other. Holidays weren't terribly significant. When I had to work a holiday my wife and I would simply celebrate on another day. It wasn't a big deal. Weekends didn't exist for me in the traditional sense. My days off occurred randomly, sometimes in the middle of the week, even in the middle of the day. Nonconformity was my normal.

I reflected on the first time I saw the victim of capital punishment by firing squad. Bullets tore through the condemned inmate's chest, isolating the heart in the process. I remember thinking about how instantaneously this person's life was taken. The very core of that person having been removed. It made quite an impression on me. I think back now on the similitude of that moment.

The news of David's death blew a hole right through the middle of me that took a part of my soul. I may never feel whole again, but I'll heal with time. I'm also reassured that I'm not alone in my grief.

The pain of those memories weighed heavily in my throat and tore at the lining of my stomach. When the world began spinning forward again, the realization of what had happened tore the aching heart out of my chest. My mind's eye finally saw clearly as if a fog of workaholism had lifted. Now that time with my brother-in-law was abruptly taken from me, time suddenly meant something.

Chapter 2
In Honor of David

David was my wife's little brother and my soul twin. He was almost seven when I met his big sister -- the love of my life. She and I began dating right away and that little guy chaperoned most of our dates. When he was older and I had a son of my own, I thanked David for being such an effective chaperone and promised to send his little nephew with him on his dates to keep him out of trouble.

We had a lot in common, which made it very easy to get along. We both enjoyed exploring the backcountry of central Utah, catching lizards, karate, biking, and Boy Scouts. Mostly, we loved playing video games. Although I had more experience with video games, he knew all the tricks and I had no chance of ever beating him.

When he was fifteen he lived with us for the summer and worked at Hogle Zoo. We had three young children and they loved having their uncle live with them. At first, it was difficult for me to imagine having a teenager in the house, but he was different from most teenagers. He was very willing to please, even at his own cost. He was also very healthy, or so we thought.

Toward the end of summer he complained of being so thirsty that he couldn't quench his thirst. He drank so much water that it caused him to have to pee every thirty minutes. Little did we know it wasn't excessive drinking that caused him to have to urinate so often. He was diagnosed with Type 1 diabetes. Even though working outside in the heat required constant hydration and his elusive medical condition created all kinds of problems for him, he went to work every day, not wanting to let anybody down for not fulfilling his responsibility.

I recall one day when I arrived at the zoo after work to pick him up as planned and I waited longer than usual. It worried me, so I called my wife to see if she had any information. I discovered that David had stayed home because he didn't feel well. When I arrived home he was very apologetic for not being where we had planned and more concerned about putting me out than his own health.

This happened a few more times, which concerned us because he was generally a very healthy boy. We suspected something was wrong, but couldn't do much about it, not being his parents. Luckily, summer break was ending soon and he would be going home where Dad could take him to see a doctor.

Well, Dad took him to see a doctor and discovered that his condition was severe enough to warrant a helicopter flight to Primary Children's Hospital.

I was at work when I received the call from my wife that David was being flown to Primary and she asked me to meet him there since the hospital was next door to my office. She wanted somebody there to meet him and she was thirty minutes away. This was not the first time David was flown to the children's hospital by helicopter.

A previous time was when he was about twelve and sustained a head injury while sledding down a dirt hill on a sheet of scrap metal. He skidded into a boulder and injured the left side of his head. We received a call from a friend who said that David was vomiting, so she took him to the emergency room where they prepared him for Life Flight to Primary Children's Hospital. Mom and Dad were traveling home and had no cell service, so Katy went to be with David until they could get turned around.

The morning my wife called me to deliver the excruciating news about David's death, her first concern was for me. Empathy for others was something she and her little brother had in common. She was frantic that I might find out about David's death by looking at my computer and she didn't want me to find out that way. If David was my soul twin, then his sister, my beautiful wife, was my soul mate.

I can't even imagine how I would have reacted to seeing David's name in my death database. Checking the computer for the day's lineup of cases was usually the first thing I did when I got to work. Surprisingly, I hadn't looked at the database at all that morning.

After the phone call, I made sure my employees were all right and then left work to go home and console my wife. Our greatest concern was what to do about our three children. When she received the call from her Dad that morning, she was in the process of dropping our seven-year-old at school. The two oldest were already at school, so they were completely unaware of the tragedy that befell our family earlier that morning. Now we worried about how to handle telling them after school.

My wife also worried about her young siblings, who still lived at home. We decided that she should drive to her parent's house and console her grieving family. It was a two-hour drive to her parent's house, so she left right away and I went back to work. The plan was that I would stay in Salt Lake City to pick the kids up from school. I would wait until later when she got back to tell them about David.

Being back at work was difficult. It was impossible for me to dissociate work from emotion so I could do my job. My heart mourned for the families of each and every patient in a way that I had never felt before. I finally left the autopsy suite and hid myself upstairs in my office for the rest of the day, all the while drowning out the pain by updating standard operating procedures and balancing purchase orders.

I left a little early so I could pick up my kids from school. I had no idea how I was going maintain composure until my wife returned home. I'm terrible at keeping secrets and I've always hated surprises. Also, I wear my emotions on my sleeve. This was the most difficult secret I ever had to keep from my kids because I was so emotional. However, keeping my mouth shut was easy compared to holding back the tears. Everything reminded me of David.

I dropped the two oldest kids off at piano lessons and my youngest helped me set up for our in-home karate class that we affectionately called, "Daddy Dojo." After the two oldest kids returned home from piano lessons we started karate class. Teaching karate that night might have been therapeutic except that karate was something that David and I had in common. He had recently joined my old karate class in Price under the direction of my Sensei. It was difficult to hold back the tears as I instructed class; I was imagining David following along.

After karate, I received a call from my wife asking us to meet her for dinner. She was driving back with her brother and sister and they wanted to eat someplace in honor of David. Since his favorite food was sushi, we decided to meet at our favorite sushi restaurant down the street from our house.

I was quiet and pensive as I drove the four miles to the restaurant. The kids talked and laughed with each other on the way, which only made it more difficult for me. It made me think about their youthful innocence and how it was going to be shattered in a matter of minutes. I thought about all the future precious moments in their life that would not include "Uncle Davey." This dinner would mark the first absence of many. I couldn't help but imagine missing him over the holidays. I almost lost it until my attention was shaken by police lights, what my kids call "blueberries," flashing in my rear view mirror.

I had just pulled into the parking lot and looked up when I noticed flashing blue and red lights coming from a police vehicle behind me. I saw a swarm of people to my left and I thought perhaps the officer was answering a call to a public disturbance or something. Nope, I was wrong. He was there for me.

The officer approached my window as I rolled it down. He asked the quintessential cop question, "Do you know why I pulled you over?"

I had no idea he was even behind me until just then, so of course I had no idea why he had pulled me over. According to the officer I turned right at a red light a few blocks back and he felt that my stop wasn't long enough. I wanted to argue with him, but I wasn't in the mood. What would I say anyway?

I wanted to say, "Hey man, look, go easy on me. My brother died today." But that wasn't entirely true, was it? He was my brother-in-law. How could I explain my brotherly bond with David and do it any justice without making me sound desperate and crazy? It was pointless trying to argue. Besides, I didn't want my kids to find out about David's death that way, so I just took the ticket and thanked the officer like it was some kind of honor. At least for a brief moment, anger and frustration replaced grief and sorrow, so I guess I could have been grateful for that.

Eventually my wife arrived and we all sat down. My seven-year-old looked around the table and asked, "Where's David?"

Distressing silence followed. The four of us who knew just looked at each other as if to say, "I'm not answering that."

My wife and I knew that our delivery of the bad news was critical and this was not the time or the place. We avoided the question for now and decided to tell them when we got back home. Thankfully nobody demanded an answer, so we skipped the uneasiness for the moment.

Throughout the day via text message and telephone conversation, we had discussed and decided upon a way to tell our kids the news that would provide a solid foundation. We hoped that this would allow us to build up to the bad news from someplace positive and strong. When we arrived home, I approached the conversation from a spiritual background in a family discussion.

I began by explaining my belief in the purpose of life. I described something greater than the kind of purpose that drives us to set goals or obtain our dream jobs. I wanted them to understand that if they believed in God, then they must also accept that he had a purpose to bring about the eternal life and exaltation of every man, woman, and child. I explained that this meant that everyone who ever lived must also die in order to achieve that goal.

We discussed life before mortality and the gift of freedom to make choices. Choosing mortality meant choosing pain and death, but it also provided a path to happiness through family bonds and true friends. I talked about baptism and other saving ordinances of the Gospel of Jesus Christ and stressed the love of God, the saving grace of Christ and the concept of forever families.

When it seemed to me that my children's tender hearts and minds were buoyed up by faith I turned the conversation over to my wife to offer the bad news. I felt it was important for her to share the news about her brother. I also trusted that she would present it with all the love and tenderness of a mother.

As my wife spoke I saw light and happiness leave my babies' eyes. There was heaviness in my chest and I felt my heart break. Faces around the room were red and shirt sleeves were bathed in snot and tears. I watched my oldest son sink deeply into the couch as if he was being swallowed by a large blue suede monster. My youngest son crawled on the floor toward his mother's lap, and that's where he sat for the rest of the night without a peep. My thirteen-year-old daughter was less expressive at first, but as she held in the tears her face swelled up like a ripened tomato, eventually popped, and she wept for the rest of the night.

Sobbing and sniffling continued throughout the house all through the night. In the morning my wife said that everybody in the house cried in their sleep all night long. Obviously, she did not sleep.

The news of David's death shattered our blissful existence. His suicide broke something in me that seemed irreparable at the time. I even considered quitting my job at the medical examiner's office. I couldn't look at another suicide victim the same way. They all reminded me of David. They all had similar stories, and they all had families who were mourning.

I felt like my position as a suicide prevention researcher was compromised. I asked myself how a person like me who had researched suicide for almost fifteen years could miss the signs in someone so close? I felt useless and ashamed as I asked myself why I couldn't save my brother!

If you're reading this book you're likely struggling with the same questions about coping with suicide that I've wrestled with for years, mysteries that have consumed the better part of my life. Dealing with David's death has helped bring to the surface some realizations.

The remaining chapters offer insight into suicidology and provide a pathway towards understanding how to cope with great loss. Each chapter will discuss one of seven proven mechanisms that have helped me cope with death and dying, not only professionally, but *personally,* with the suicide death of my brother-in-law.

Chapter 3
Chainmail Armor

Many years ago I worked as a volunteer EMT/firefighter. I carried a bag of first aid tools in my vehicle. I called the bag my 'jump-kit' because it was easy to grab in a hurry and it allowed me to quickly jump into action and save lives. My hope for you is that by the end of this book you will have your very own 'virtual jump-kit' full of tools that will help you cope and spare your anguish in the wake of tragedy.

The remainder of the book is structured into six sections that outline seven unique coping strategies. Each strategy or mechanism can be practiced individually or combined for greater efficacy. The seven strategies include: Consistency, Choice, Courage, Camaraderie, Comfort, Communication, and Charity. Each of these seven concepts or strategies listed above can be a tool in your jump-kit just like the life-saving tools in my emergency first-aid jump-kit.

I must warn you, just as I went through training in order to learn how to effectively use each of the life-saving tools in my jump-kit, you must learn how to use each of the strategies discussed in this book. It's not enough to know about something, you need to put forth the effort to understand it enough in order to practice the concept effectively. Each coping mechanism can be practiced independently, however, when interwoven; their power to heal is increased exponentially.

This idea of intricate connections reminds me of a project that my brother-in-law started several years ago. His love of fantasy stories and video games encouraged him to create a chainmail shirt. He spent hours cutting wire and curling tiny metal rings. He left the rings open so they were in a C-shape. After he assembled a collection of several thousand rings he began connecting them by pinching each ring closed around the next in a very elaborate pattern. He wasn't able to complete the shirt, but before he died he had an impressive piece woven together.

Chainmail armament protected medieval warriors from being pierced by arrows. Today, I use cut proof gloves while performing autopsies. They are not metal, but they remind me of chainmail in that they protect my hands from being cut by a scalpel blade.

By design, each of the coping mechanisms discussed in this book begin with the letter 'C.' As you read each chapter and develop a strategy around each concept that fits your circumstance, I want you to imagine C-shaped rings closing around each other and connecting in a way to create an impenetrable force as with chainmail. I encourage you to do the same with each of the coping strategies. Most importantly, I need you to understand that none of these mechanisms should be practiced as "one-and-done." You must endure and continue to practice the strategies you've developed. Albeit impressive, David's piece of woven metal couldn't protect him because it's incomplete.

Commit to yourself to complete the following three tasks today: First, read this book; Second, personalize each coping strategy; Third, practice your personalized strategy. Every time you use a coping strategy to get you through a rough moment you connect another ring in your chainmail armor. The more complete your armor, the better equipped you'll be to defend against adversarial thoughts and feelings. These thoughts and feelings come from a dark place and sometimes come without warning. They can deeply wound you if your armor is incomplete, so continually work on building your armor.

I've created a graphic that will aid you in tracking your progress. You can find this graphic and other useful resources at www.linksofcourage.com.

Color in a C-shaped piece of chainmail every time you practice one of your strategies. If you're diligent in practicing your strategies, you will begin to see a difference in your mood and an improved ability to ward off bad feelings.

- CONSISTENCY -

Chapter 4
Maintaining Normalcy

The first coping strategy I want to discuss is consistency. Consistency after loss by suicide is important for several reasons. First of all, your world has been turned upside-down and you need an anchor to hold you right-side up. Changing routine now will only further set you back. Secondly, having something consistent to turn to will ensure that you don't stray down dark paths, and it will provide a beacon to guide you back in case you do get lost. The next three chapters will provide insight into the concept of consistency.

Our society is very gracious and compassionate when it comes to the death of a loved one. Most companies offer grievance leave, airlines and hotels might offer discounts, and teachers will provide passes for missed homework assignments. These peace offerings appear as light in the darkness, but the truth of the matter is they can be detrimental, depending upon how they are received.

After all, they are simply temporary patches that will only get you through the first few days following tragedy. The problem with these benefits is that if you use them as a crutch in order to take more time off work or more time out of school than you genuinely need you might find yourself in an endless loop of grief.

The day my children lost their uncle to suicide I struggled with what to do. I thought about taking them out of school immediately. Having them home would have certainly made me feel better, but that would not have been the best option for them. Instead, we chose not to interrupt their normal routine.

We allowed them to finish the day as usual and created an opportunity to share the news later in the evening after our Monday routine played out as planned. Surprisingly, the very next day our brave little son asked his mother if he could go to school. Of course, with a request like that, she had no argument. He went to school readily and happily just like every other day. He returned home with the same exuberance. His behavior seemed so abnormal given the circumstances that we worried something was deeply wrong with our little guy, but it wasn't. Eventually he opened up when he was ready.

To better understand my son's behavior, I consulted a pediatric psychiatrist. I had worked with this trusted friend and colleague as a research assistant for many years and as expected he have me sound advice.

He told me that when a child experiences loss the most important thing a parent can do is maintain normalcy. Going through the motions was a safe bet. The take-home lesson from our discussion was that when a child sensed that a loss had adversely affected them personally, and then they would perceive the loss as an even greater tragedy if their life was directly affected and would never be the same.

Two words stood out in my mind, "Maintain normalcy."

Although my family took the customary days off and eventually began professional counseling, we did not hesitate to get back to our normal routines as soon as possible. The most difficult activity ended up being the most therapeutic and rewarding-- trick-or-treating on Halloween.

My wife's favorite holiday has always been Halloween. She grew up hosting spook alleys and haunted houses for County Recreation. She had continued the tradition by hosting spooky parties in our home. Our friends and neighbors have come to anticipate a Halloween block party at my house every year. Spooky and haunted was normal for my family.

Her emotions told her to forget celebrating Halloween this year, mostly because her wound was fresh and it felt inappropriate to be celebrating so soon. However, we discussed how important it was for our kids to don their costumes that they had worked on so diligently and then walk around the neighborhood to show them off to their friends.

We decided that we couldn't afford not to celebrate, so we did. This was an example of being consistent, which paid off in the end. If we hadn't celebrated I'd hate to think that my kids might have held resentment toward David for ruining their holiday. It was bad enough that they would have to learn how to forgive him for leaving them so abruptly.

As we walked up and down every side street in our neighborhood with our little Galaxy Guardians and

Witchy Poo, I felt a calming peace with every mile. My wife's youngest brother joined our eclectic group of trick-or-treaters. His version of Star Lord fit naturally with my sons' Groot and Rocket costumes. We explored parts of our neighborhood that were a new frontier for me. Maybe it was just the reverent way in which we were carrying ourselves, but it felt other-worldly to me like how I imagine space exploration-quiet and serene. We were extending ourselves and it felt different and good all at the same time.

The weather was unusually pleasant and warm for late October in Utah. Even the occasional wind that usually nipped at our noses was calm and inviting. This was the first year the kids could actually show off their costumes instead of hiding them under parkas.

There was nothing magical or mystical about that night, even though it was Halloween. The fact that we decided to act normal and stick with the program established the possibility that things could be normal. Going through the motions, so to speak, allowed me to reflect appropriately and process what had happened five days earlier.

I saw a glimmer of hope in my children's eyes as they ran back from each door with their trick-or-treating spoils. I hadn't seen their eyes glisten for several days, and to see the excitement in them now was magical.

Someone we loved had died and it left emptiness in our lives. That emptiness was a painful, gaping void that we desperately wanted to fill with something in order to minimize the discomfort. I was very cautious about what filled that space, so I began journaling my recovery. As I went back and read some of my entries, I discovered something. Although I took a few days off work for funeral services and changed my schedule a little bit to accommodate my grieving family, my daily activities didn't change. Even some of our big family events carried on as planned. I noticed the tone of my writing brighten up as the weeks grew into months.

My recommendation to you is to begin journaling your experience. Put your emotions on paper and record your progress. If your feelings at first are explicit, then write them down on a piece of paper and destroy the paper afterwards. They are not for anyone else to read. It's very therapeutic to get the words out and then throw them away and forget about them.

Thoughts and Impressions

Chapter 5
Consistency Is a Direct Route to Healing

I've found that consistency is a more direct path to healing. The key is to keep moving and look ahead.

As we walked home from trick-or-treating, I was reminded of the day when I was so happy for my son as he learned to ride his bicycle up the same street in our quiet little neighborhood. It was not without constant pedaling and a consistent reminder to look up.

I remember taking turns with my wife holding on to his seat and running beside him as he wibble-wobbled up and down the sidewalk. I thought he looked like a ping-pong ball bouncing from one side to the other.

I would push for a while and then let go as he shouted, "Dad, don't let go!" His voice trailed for a few yards until he looked back and swerved side to side, eventually toppling over onto the neighbor's grass.

No matter how carefully I would let go of his seat he had an extrasensory perception that knew every time. Fear inevitably set in and he would look around at all the obstacles that he now needed to navigate alone and he would stop pedaling. Almost instantaneously his balance was thrown off and he tipped over. Overcoming his fear of doing it alone was his first hurdle. More importantly, he needed to keep pedaling.

When he finally got over his fear of going alone and kept pedaling, he stayed up for a bit longer. However, very soon his spinning feet and the ground moving beneath him would capture his attention and he veered into every obstacle along his path, whether it was shrubbery or a fence or simply the edge of the sidewalk. When he was lucky he'd fall onto the neighbor's spongy, manicured lawn.

As he began to look down, I would holler to 'look forward,' but there was nothing I could do except scurry to his side after he crashed. As I lifted him up and brushed him off, I reminded him to keep pedaling, look up and watch where he was going.

He had to master two things before he could ride straight down the sidewalk without crashing. First, he had to continue to pedal by letting go of his fear of moving forward alone. Second, he needed to look up and straight ahead in order to keep from crashing into things.

After you experience a loss, people may tell you that you seem like you're just going through the motions, but that's okay! Take that as a good sign. Don't let that stop you. Keep moving forward. Think of consistency as a code word for going through the motions. Remember that maintaining normalcy is important.

The next step in moving forward is to discover your stumbling blocks and remove them one by one so they can't hold you back. Set a reachable goal that will help you to move forward.

You might think that going through the motions feels an awful lot like treading water. When you feel like you're going nowhere and decide to stop treading is when you drown. Just like when my son stopped pedaling, he crashed. Symbolically speaking, kicking your feet and flapping your arms can be tiring and might leave you feeling hopeless, but if you keep moving it will eventually pay off. If done right, you will develop metaphorical muscles that will allow you to pull yourself up and out of the mire.

If you have no place to look in front of you then you'll be drawn to the past. You will turn to memories which will take you on a downward spiral that may be difficult to pull out of. Defining a goal in front of you will provide a destination. A realistic goal will be the impetus that drives you forward and forces you to look up.

The days following David's death were difficult. Adding to the tribulation was the need to pore over old photographs and memorabilia in order to create a memoriam for his funeral. I was tempted to go through everything in his room and learn every little nuance that I didn't already know. I could have stayed there for a very long time. It was comfortable, but it was also damaging to my progress.

I remember at one point my wife had the impression to hand over everything to a close friend. He agreed to create a video montage of memories so that we could focus on other things. We realized later that it was the right decision. It allowed us to move forward, and our friend created a beautiful memorial video.

The family had to get past another hurdle regarding funeral services. There were two overarching opinions that needed to be discussed and decided upon. Some of us thought that a small memorial for family and close friends was appropriate, while others felt that no service at all was the best option, given the idea that David would have preferred no service.

It was a very easy decision to be faced with compared to others, but more importantly, it gave us something to work toward. It kept us moving and thinking rather than stagnating over old photographs and memories.

We decided upon a small gathering of family and close friends with a display table of David's memorabilia. The *piece de resistance* was the video montage that our friend put together of every photograph we had gathered depicting David's life.

Miraculously, the small college seminary building that we booked for the quaint memoriam maxed the room's capacity limit. Friends and family filled the room and spilled out into the foyer. They enjoyed looking at Legend of Zelda memorabilia, Rubik's puzzles of all shapes and sizes, Boy Scout paraphernalia, and countless other trinkets that told the story of David Taylor.

It was a sight to behold and very therapeutic to experience such an outpouring of love and compassion from his community. As a family, we were grateful that we had gone through the motions and followed through with an event that could have easily been avoided.

You are going to be overwhelmed. That is to be expected. Don't let your pride or your traditions dictate your current situation. Don't allow fear or uncertainty to govern your decisions. Don't be afraid to ask for help, and for goodness' sake, don't push away help when it's offered. Allow others the privilege of serving you. Someday they'll need your help and then you can repay the favor.

Whether you choose a memorial service that includes family and closest friends gathered in your living room around an urn or whether you rent an arena, it will be important for you to experience the appreciation that others have for your loved one. That perspective will settle down in your soul and become a light you can turn to in the darkness.

Chapter 6
Looking Upward and Ahead

People will advise you to take time off and get away from it all. You may want to avoid daily routine as you grieve. This is not the best direction to take. Remember, consistency is a more direct path to healing. The key is to look upward and ahead.

Believe me, when my world fell apart, I wanted to press pause on life and rewind to a happier time. I was tempted to play the "director's cut" of my life and review highlights. Looking back at the "good times" was supposed to feel good, but it didn't. It hurt even deeper than I expected. That's when I realized that remembering happy times could only make me happy after I was mentally prepared for it.

If you replay the happy memories too soon you'll wind up in an endless loop of sorrow and regret, turning to something meant to bring comfort, but finding only hurt. You might think that looking back and remembering good times will help you cope with the death of your loved one, but if you're not mentally prepared to revisit those memories, the images will haunt you and will tear your heart out.

It's easier said than done, right. Don't worry, this concept seemed counterintuitive to me too, until I practiced the principle and discovered the truth behind it.

I am not telling you to forget your loved one and move on, but when your mind is stuck on sadness, all you remember is pain. You need a goal and a purpose in order to press forward and you need to look straight ahead in order to find that purpose. This will take your mind to a healthy place where you will be able to return to happier memories.

You may have considered looking upward as a call for guidance from a higher power on a spiritual level, or you may have considered the call to look forward as an opportunity to set goals. In either case, it is essential that you establish a purpose, or at least a plan of action. This follows the same course of action my son took when he established an attainable goal of staying up on his bike for at least a few yards at a time, all the while pedaling his little heart out.

I told you that on the day I received news of my brother-in-law's death I left work to go home and console my wife. I was tempted to stay home, look at family pictures, and sob alone after she had left, but instead I did something unexpected. I dumbfounded my coworkers by returning to work and finishing my daily routine. It wasn't easy, but I needed something to keep my mind busy so it wouldn't take me down darker paths.

The decision to return to work and leave the kids in school provided consistency and we hoped that decision would help preserve our children's innocence a little longer. We knew that the news of David's death would rob them of that.

Keeping that secret while we went through our normal Monday routine was an excruciating experience, but I knew it was critical. Also, going back to work made better sense than sitting home alone. Little did I know, that was my first step toward healing.

When we were all finally back together later that evening, we followed through with our usual family night. As mentioned earlier, we didn't just tell our children the news of their uncle's death, but first prepared them to hear the news. After the news had sunk in, we discussed a plan for moving forward.

Part of our family's plan was to continue talking about David as usual, without hesitation or fear of upsetting anyone. We committed ourselves to maintaining his legacy by continuing some of his goals. In essence, we had committed to maintaining normalcy by incorporating some of David's practices into our daily routine.

Instead of fixating on past memories and focusing on what we had lost, we looked forward and pressed onward with a purpose and a plan to involve David's ideals in our daily life. Rather than being lost to us, David was now more a part of our lives than ever before. We hadn't continued doing something that was normal for us; instead we adopted and preserved a habit of David's that was a normal practice for him.

Maintaining normalcy and being consistent doesn't have to confine you to your old daily routine. Commit today to create a legacy for your lost loved one as we did with David by adopting his charitable ideals. Most importantly, don't stop. As you maintain continuity and consistency, you will soon be able to remember your loved one with veneration rather than desperation.

- CHOICE -

Chapter 7
Your Environment Matters

The next coping strategy I want to discuss is choice. Before I continue, I need you to understand something about choice. With choice comes accountability. Let me explain. It's true that your choices are influenced by your environment, but the reverse is also true. Your environment is shaped by your choices. The next three chapters will explain this concept.

I'm no stranger to death. I've seen how a person's environment has led to their death, especially suicide. I've also seen how one suicide has influenced another, especially in families and small communities. Of course, suicide is more complicated than that. There are a myriad of associated factors involved with suicide, but I want to focus on this idea of choice.

My outlook on life has changed since my brother-in-law's death. This new perspective has caused me to see the world through a different filter. I've researched suicide for the past fifteen years, but this time I've chosen to allow it to affect me.

I used to watch shows where people would make gestures of killing themselves and never gave it a second thought. At times I would even chuckle when people made gestures, like putting an imaginary gun to their head or pulling upward on an imaginary rope as if to hang themselves. I knew they were just acting out a script that was exaggerating a bad situation. No big deal, right? It wasn't a big deal for me until now. Now when I see somebody make a suicidal gesture, I become greatly concerned. I wonder if they truly appreciate the impulsive choice they had just displayed.

I remember just days after David's death we were all sitting in the front room relaxing and watching TV. A show came on with a character named David. I had never before been as aware of a name being used so much in such a short period of time than on this television show this particular night. Eerily, it felt as if David himself was attempting to contact us from beyond the grave. It was uncomfortable, but that wasn't the worst of it. There was a point in the drama when another character said, "David, why don't you just kill yourself?"

I carefully looked around the room, checking for signs of distress at this ill-timed comment. Under the circumstances that comment was more offensive to me than any four-letter obscenity. My father-in-law quickly changed the channel and tossed the remote to me.

I thought about the sadness of that moment and the commentary it offered on today's society. All too often we coast through life and allow ourselves to be bombarded with offensive slang and irreverent comments. We've chosen to accept it as normal, as if our society has become addicted to rudeness.

Reflecting back on the story I shared earlier about my son's success in riding his bicycle, I learned a great lesson about the choices we make. I also realized that it didn't happen overnight. In fact, he did not learn how to ride his bicycle for several weeks. He experienced many failures. Each attempt required a little more encouragement than the last.

I had a responsibility as his mentor to pick him up and put him back on the bike, but he had a responsibility to choose to continue trying. He chose not to obsess on his failures nor dwell on the pain of road rash when he crashed. I didn't need to hold on forever either, but I did need to stand by, encourage and celebrate each success with him.

He could have reviewed the highlights and bloopers in his mind and decide that the pain was too much to handle and never hop on his bicycle again. Instead, he chose to look forward with determination that he would get back on the bike and keep on pedaling.

In the end, it had nothing to do with me. I was just there to pick him up occasionally when the pressure was too great for him to pick himself up. It boiled down to the fact that he had a decision to make and I couldn't make it for him. He combined choice and consistency and found success.

An obvious dichotomy exists. It seems to me that for every person out there fighting to stay alive there is somebody fighting to die. I do not condone or promote suicide; however, I do acknowledge freedom of choice. I want to point out that as you cope with the suicide of a loved one you must choose to forgive their choice. You must also allow yourself grace to forgive yourself.

The most prevalent difficulty that I see for a lot of families who are dealing with the loss of a loved one is getting past two questions: "Why," and "What more could I have done?"

The medical examiner can offer answers to questions of how somebody died or when they died, but the answer to the question of why they died is complicated. As a suicide researcher I've interviewed hundreds of families in an attempt to answer questions related to contributing factors that might be associated with suicide, but even the extrapolation of my results can't answer the question of why they chose death over life.

Even suicide notes don't provide comfort in understanding "why." Most departure notes are philosophical in nature and apologetic. Very few offer solace or understanding. Most are simply an accounting of personal belongings and to whom they should be given.

The bottom line is that you must choose to move past the unanswered questions, the blame and the guilt. There's no going backwards. This was a concept that was very difficult for me to accept at first. I wanted to know why David made this devastating decision. And, albeit beautiful and poetic, his suicide note did not offer answers.

Whatever pain and anguish he was going through, I had to accept that suicide was his answer to peace. My answer to peace came when I finally let go of my guilt and accepted that I had no control over his choice.

Chapter 8
How Do You Cope With Death?

I would like to set the stage a little better to help you understand my perspective as a scientist. I work at the medical examiner's office that operates in a central lab in Salt Lake City. Its jurisdiction includes the entire state of Utah. Utah law defines the types of deaths that are reported to the medical examiner's office and those which require a forensic autopsy.

As defined by law, the medical examiner is responsible for all unattended deaths, homicides, suicides, drug overdoses, infants and children, accidents including traffic deaths and recreational deaths. OME investigates thousands of cases per year, with over 2,500 actually being examined at the central office in Salt Lake City.

A recent study conducted by the University of Utah in conjunction with the medical examiner reviewed over 600 possible suicides during a 1-year period. Interviews with family members were conducted during that year in order to understand the circumstances surrounding each death. It was determined that only about 40% of the "possible suicides" received a final manner of death that were declared a 'Suicide.' Without definitive evidence to support an intentional death the medical examiner will rule the death as 'Undetermined.'

Over the past 20 years, researchers at the University of Utah have looked objectively at genetic analysis, genealogical data, and environmental factors such as air quality and altitude, but the most valuable lessons I've learned have come from talking to families left behind.

I've learned two irrefutable things. First, and foremost, it was therapeutic for families to talk about their dearly departed. It gave them an opportunity to paint a softer picture of their loved one. Second, some people had been saved after previous attempts through therapy and medication, but inevitably they still made the choice to die. There might had been a myriad of reasons why a person took their own life, but ultimately it boiled down to one final act that was so devastating there was no way to save them.

As a manager I've interviewed many people wanting to work for the medical examiner's office. Some have legitimate reasons, but most are looking to satisfy their morbid curiosity. In order to vet out legitimate contenders, I ask several very important questions, paying special attention to how they respond to the following question, "How do you cope with death and dying?"

The following response is consistent among successful recruits. "I accept that death is a natural part of life. It's not easy, but it's necessary."

What I've observed over the past 15 years is that those who have successfully coped with the death of a loved one are well-adjusted and have continued on to great things. They've accepted that tragedy happens to everyone and is not the plot in some cosmic scheme to make them suffer personally.

Bad things happen to everyone equally. Every living person on this earth will die at some point. It's the very state of mortality. You create a problem for yourself when you focus on the pain and suffering of those you value most. You shut out the rest of the world and self-preservation kicks in, causing you to turn inward. This inward reflection focusses the pain of your tragedy like a beam of light through a magnifying glass. You tend to forget everyone else around you, thus making it seem like all the tragedy in the world is focused on you.

I don't mean to diminish your pain and suffering. I appreciate that it's real, but I'm suggesting that if you want to end your suffering you must first make a choice to accept death as a natural part of life. Once you've done that, then you can focus on where your pain is really coming from.

Read the next example, at the end of the story I'll pinpoint for you the origin of my pain.

My wife and I visited her family about a week before David's death. Our trip was unplanned and a complete surprise. We stopped by unannounced and caught the family doing whatever it is people do when they are not anticipating visitors. There were no expectations. I'll never forget the experience. It will always be one of my most treasured memories.

David was in the middle of building an apparatus to study the physics of light. He read about a double-slit experiment and wanted to see the results for himself. Being a lover of science myself, I couldn't help but jump in.

We gathered a few tools such as a piece of paper, aluminum foil, tape, and a fine tip razor blade. The easy part was taping foil in the middle of the paper. The most difficult part was cutting two equal slits in the foil-covered paper. We spent 30 minutes and went through several pieces of paper before we created something that would work.

I'll never forget his jubilance the moment he pointed the light source at the two slits in the foil-wrapped paper and saw a pattern of light appear on the opposite wall. I held the light in place while he quickly outlined the interference pattern on the wall.

He was so excited that he began gathering every light source he could find and pointing each one at the double slits. He came up with three different patterns using three different colored laser pointers. He thought it was amazing that a single beam of light could be split into so many different patterns. What we saw that night was the interaction of individual photons and how their environment directed them to behave differently.

My pain came from the timing of David's death. He was so young that all I could think about was all the lost time and missed opportunities that lay ahead. When I started thinking about the lost time I had to force myself to remember the plan that my family established right away on the very night of his death. Our plan was simple. We chose to continue to talk about him, to explore new things in his honor, and to continue his legacy of giving. Once I remembered that, I was able to look to the destination and focus on my family's goal of continuing David's legacy. Something amazing happened! Suddenly, those opportunities weren't lost.

Something else remarkable happened. As I slowly turned outward, so did the beam of light that was focused so painfully inward. No longer was it laser-focused on my heart burning a hole through my soul. I opened up and allowed the light to shine on those around me.

Friends, my desire for writing this book comes from a good place. I certainly don't understand all mysteries, nor do I feel I have all knowledge, but I hope my story can reach many who are struggling and help them find peace like I have. I hope you choose to continue reading so you may someday see yourself clearly as others see you. You are strong-willed, valuable, and capable of being happy again.

If you are struggling with the loss of a loved one, choose today to do two things: First, accept your struggle, and then find a friend to help you work through the rough times.

Chapter 9
Choosing To Sink or Swim

Until I chose to move past the unanswered questions, the blame and the guilt, my soul was weighed down by a tremendous amount of guilt. While I didn't feel like I had a part to play in David's death, rather I beat myself up asking what I could have done to prevent it.

A few months later a new type of guilt shocked my heart when I noticed that his parents and siblings seemed to be coping but I was still a blubbering fool. I thought to myself, "How dare I sulk when his own mother was smiling again. Who was I to be so sad?"

My heart was heavy and I needed answers, so I turned to the words of my mentor. I remembered asking him how I could have missed the signs after all these years of studying suicide and investigating so many cases. Now, his response resounded more clearly in my mind.

This is important. I want you to understand this concept. This is how I took control of myself and continued down the road to recovery. If I had missed this concept I would have been stalled somewhere between bargaining and denial, dwelling on something I had no control over.

Hindsight is always more clear than foresight. As I thought about all the supposed triggers associated with suicide, I could list all of David's very easily after the fact. It was simple to place him into those categories now that he had already made his decision. It was like working a maze from the finish line.

I tried to imagine being in a situation with David where I actually saw one of the triggers. I asked myself whether or not I would have naturally jumped to the conclusion that he would harm himself. That's when I realized that although years of research had uncovered a lot of ideas about suicidology, there was nothing concrete to say that if a person exhibits one of these characteristics then they will commit suicide. That just isn't so.

David and I thought so much alike I had never considered that suicide was an option no matter what trial he was facing. I had seen him overcome great obstacles in his life. Even his successes were ultimately out of my control. I could support him and encourage him, but in the end he had to make a choice in every one of those situations.

When I finally accepted the fact that David made a choice that was completely out of my hands, I was able to move past my guilt and respect his decision. However, overcoming the guilt of feeling unworthy to grieve came much later.

Almost a year after David's death, my wife and I ran an obstacle course race at Lake Tahoe, California. The race was 15 miles long and had about 40 obstacles along its path. One of those obstacles required swimming 100 yards across a frozen pond.

Most people avoided swimming by doing 60 burpees instead. Those of us who braved the frigid waters fell into three categories: those who admitted failure immediately and climbed back out of the pond, those who failed midway and needed to be rescued, and those who finished.

Although I finished, I did not finish as quickly or as gracefully as my wife, who flew through the water like a mermaid. I remember feeling like I was literally frozen in time and space. It didn't seem to matter how hard I kicked my legs or flapped my arms, the shoreline stood still and my wife moved farther and farther away from me. I was swimming so hard I should have been flying.

I looked around and saw people being pulled out of the water one by one onto small boats. Rescuers on the boats were ready to wrap the cold contestant in silver space blankets. One lady directly beside me was crying outwardly as hard as I was crying inwardly. She finally gave up and rolled onto her back so her husband could drag her across the lake. I believed that although my progress was slower than my wife's, all I needed to do was continue swimming. If I had stopped, my muscles would have seized and I would literally have been dead in the water. Eventually I made it to the other side.

I compared the struggle in my mind of wanting to give up and to be pulled out of the tormenting icy waters to the overwhelming feeling of trying to swim but drowning instead. It helped me appreciate the fight David had for finding freedom at whatever cost.

Comparatively, coping with the death of a loved one is like learning how to fly underwater. Although you're going through the same motions of flapping your arms to stay afloat, you're really not flying at all. If you were truly flying you would be soaring above the clouds, feeling the wind comb through your hair as you watched the ground rush past beneath you. Flying evokes a sense of freedom.

Instead, you're going through the motions, but no billowy clouds nor rushing wind, only the frigid depths of a vast sea of pain and doubt with ominous darkness looming below.

However, there is hope, as long as you keep swimming. Look up, see the shimmer of light dancing on the surface of the water? Set a goal and focus on your glimmer of hope. Choose to lift your head above the water and keep on flapping. You will build and strengthen the appropriate metaphorical muscles that will set you free.

- COURAGE AND CAMARADERIE -

Chapter 10
When Conquering Obstacles You Need Courage and a Champion

The next three chapters will focus on two topics that go hand-in-hand: courage and camaraderie. This coping strategy is probably the most difficult to practice because it requires you to be honest with yourself and to trust somebody else. A champion will help you out in a pinch, but it takes courage to act. It takes courage to forgive. It takes courage to accept the truth even when the truth hurts. It also takes courage to accept help.

At the break of dawn and again at the close of day I see something inspiring sitting on my night table. It's a three-piece medallion that I earned by competing in a series of obstacle course races. It has green, red, and blue pie-shaped pieces snuggled together like a pizza-shaped puzzle in a round metal plaque. Together all three tokens create the image of a gladiator helmet. Engraved around the edge of the plaque are affirmations that greet me triumphantly twice a day. The words of encouragement that I focus on are: courage and camaraderie.

A phenomenon of various obstacle course races has swept our nation over the past decade. My family has recently become addicted to the fervor. My sister's husband introduced me to one such extraordinary event last spring. He had planned on gathering a group of colleagues together to use the race as a group development tool. Little did we know this would become our new life venture.

This particular event was comprised of three distinct individual races all run at different times. The most challenging of the three was about 15 miles long and required competitors to complete over 40 obstacles. The mid-challenge race consisted of 12 miles worth of obstacles to overcome. The least challenging race was about five miles long with 20 to 30 obstacles spattered along the trail.

One constant throughout all three races was a series of walls. These walls ranged from six feet to eight feet high and about 30 feet across. There were no ropes, no ladders, and nothing to step off to assist racers over the wall. It required long arms, a good vertical leap, and powerful upper body strength.

In preparation for the race we learned that one of the tips to a successful climb required a swimming pool. It was suggested that in order to build the proper muscles to conquer the wall you should repetitively pull yourself up and out of a swimming pool. The motion of pulling yourself up and over the wall was similar.

Imagine yourself as a competitor in this race. Would you have the upper body strength to pull yourself up and over the wall? Would your vertical leap and outstretched hands reach eight feet? If so, then would you have the courage to let go on the other side? Most importantly, would you have the strength to do it alone?

Imagine my dismay when all my preparation did not overcome my limited vertical leap. My outstretched arms would not even reach the top of that damn wall. If I could have just grabbed the top of the wall I might have had enough upper body strength to pull myself up and over, but I couldn't even reach the top.

I had prepared for this. I had built the appropriate muscles, but at this point I couldn't do it alone. I must have looked quite helpless and pathetic jumping again and again, failing each time. At one point I even ran and jumped and tried to kick off the wall to add a little height, but to no avail. My outstretched arms still couldn't bridge the horizontal distance that the kick-off created just the same as it couldn't overcome the vertical distance. I simply wasn't made to scale an eight foot wall.

I knew what to expect and I had trained for it, but now I was just upset and angry at myself for failing. Even more upsetting was the consequence awaiting me for failing the obstacle. Each obstacle was assigned a volunteer who monitored the challenge, and when a competitor failed, they were asked to step aside and complete 30 burpees.

Now, I'm telling you, burpees are of the devil. I hate burpees like most people hate morning commute.

The volunteer at the wall approached me after my fourth attempt. Contempt grew in my heart for that man as he stepped closer. I stood solid and angry as I awaited my consequence, but what he said to me changed my attitude for the rest of the race. It changed my perspective.

He did not command me like a drill instructor to step aside and give me 30 burpees as I had expected. Instead he hollered, "Help your teammates!"

Hallelujah! Praise the challenge judge. What a marvelous concept. I looked around and noticed that others were struggling around me. I wasn't the only one. I accepted my vulnerability and immediately connected with others going through the same struggle.

As with any competition, training was crucial for survival. Building the appropriate muscles for strength and stamina was critical, but I realized that there was more to it than preparation. I learned a valuable lesson at that epic 15 mile race in Lake Tahoe, California. I learned that I didn't have to struggle alone.

Suddenly I wasn't worried about the pending doom of 20 more obstacles. The competitive drive that had pushed me along for the first half of the race was now replaced with another motivation. I was offered the possibility to assist and to be assisted. My previous competitors were now my teammates.

After crossing the finish line I received my medal. It wasn't first place, but it meant something more to me than excellence in competition. It carried with it perspective and an excellence in attitude, so to speak. Along with the medal came a token, one-third of a larger medallion of what race finishers call a trifecta. Each token fits together to make a much larger medallion that now sits on my night table as a reminder that I can accomplish anything when I have the courage to ask for help.

Throughout the race I was faced with many obstacles that I could accomplish on my own because of my hours of preparation and conditioning. However, I was grateful to know that I could count on a friend to help me overcome the ones that I couldn't accomplish on my own.

After the Lake Tahoe race I asked emergency responders at the event how many people they rescued off the course. I was astonished at how many competitors did not finish the race. They told me that over 300 people were carted off the mountain due to injury, and due to the fact that many of them were not prepared for the conditions.

I'll give you an idea of the conditions at this particular race. We started at a lower elevation of 6,000 feet with temperatures around 50 degrees Fahrenheit. We ascended a mountain for about seven miles to a final height of just over 9,000 feet. Near the top of the mountain we swam across a frozen pond before descending through sheets of sleet as it poured from the dismal sky.

Without something to keep warm many racers suffered hypothermia. At one point my wife and I huddled together to squeeze out the cold. If it hadn't been for the warm embrace we might have suffered the same fate as the 300 that were carried off the mountain by rescuers.

As I reflected on my experience, I thought about the courage it took to even step foot on the race track. I thought about the competitive drive that pushed me forward even through the toughest obstacles. I was grateful that camaraderie saved me when the going got tough.

Chapter 11
It Had Nothing to Do With You

For those of you who embrace the concept of camaraderie and have been someone's champion, the idea of not shouldering responsibility may be difficult for you to accept. When you've acted as somebody's cheerleader for a long time, it can be difficult to see them fail. You feel obligated to share the blame. That might stand true for some things, but not in the case of suicide. You had nothing to do with your loved one's decision to commit suicide.

For a long time, I didn't understand why my brother-in-law took his own life. I thought about all the children in the world fighting various diseases and the doctors and researchers toiling to discover cures. Yet here was a young man who had survived so much and had so much life ahead of him who still chose to end it.

I thought for sure it had something to do with the way I treated him. I suddenly felt guilty for every time I might have been impatient or condescending. I revisited in my mind every interaction, searching for that pivotal moment that made David feel less important and unworthy to live. I couldn't find that life-changing moment in our history and I certainly couldn't see it with others in the family. He was loved.

When I was younger I considered the act of taking one's life heinous and selfish, but I was wrong and it's taken me a long time to discover the truth. As much as I didn't understand the act of suicide and as much as I wanted to blame myself for not preventing David's suicide, I had to accept that his decision had nothing to do with me.

All too often we attempt to connect to our lost loved ones by blaming ourselves for the tragedy or somehow trying to play the martyr by accepting some fabricated guilt in our own minds. If you remember nothing else from this book I want you to remember this next point. If you want to cope with the loss of your love one, you must have the courage to accept this lesson: *It's not about you.* You are not to blame for the suicide death of your loved one. It's much easier to understand if you accept that it was not about you.

I've noticed that people attempt to understand things that are outside their understanding by implicating themselves. They dive right in and try to shoulder the responsibility as if somehow it will make everything better. There is a thought that somehow it will bring meaning to a meaningless thing.

As difficult as it was for me to admit, my brother-in-law made a decision to end his life. I had nothing to do with that decisions and I had to accept that it wasn't done out of a selfish need to punish somebody. The only thing I needed to do was to forgive him.

Over time, it's settled more deeply in my mind that suicide can be viewed in some ways as an act of courage. While I know this point-of-view is controversial, I'd like to consider it for a moment while discussing the following points.

Courage can mean a lot of things. When I talk about courage I tend to associate it with bravery. I imagine a warrior holding a shiny blade triumphantly in the air to begin an epic battle. I also imagine a firefighter running into a burning building to save a complete stranger. Maybe you saw a military soldier dressed in uniform. In any case, hold on to that image and explore with me what it means to be brave or to act courageously.

Our minds betray us by telling us to act a certain way based on societal norms. We bottle up our emotions and work so hard to portray the false image we want others to see. Might I suggest that bravery is allowing ourselves to be free? Courage is required in order to be honest with ourselves and break boundaries. Be brave enough to be vulnerable.

When I was young I loved to read the story of David and Goliath. I loved it! Who doesn't like a good "triumph of the underdog" story?

Not only was the story of David beating Goliath a classic tale of man versus man where good triumphed evil, but it was much more. It's taken me a long time and many personal losses to see the deeper meaning in that classic tale.

The boy, David, was somebody relatable. He was kind and thoughtful and courageous. I picked this analogy because the hero shared my brother-in-law's name, but also because it depicted a normal human being who conquered his fears.

He was bold and courageous and his moral compass was straight and narrow. He showed great faith in a higher power and defended his God no matter the consequence. More importantly, he trusted in his Lord to help him when the going got tough.

Goliath, on the other hand, represented everything wrong with the world. He was big and scary and was celebrated as a powerful warrior, but he was overconfident. His pride was his downfall.

David's courage eventually led to his victory. However, his story brought on a whole new meaning for me as I read it recently. When I was young it spoke to me about expressing faith in God and having courage to overcome great trial and tribulation. Now, as I read the story, it speaks to me about having the courage to act in the face of doubt and fear.

Courage is more than bravery and winning battles, it's stepping outside our own comfort and at times our own safety to rescue others in need. As debatable as it sounds, sometimes it means freeing ourselves from our own demons by whatever means necessary.

I started writing my story as a form of therapy in hopes of freeing myself from my demons. Eventually I realized the potential my story had of helping others. I decided to share the perspective I see every day. I wanted to give you a point of view that you might have never considered, but one that might help you get unstuck. The biggest hurdle was finding the courage to share my story with others. After all, there's a lot of personal insight and heartache poured into these pages.

Once I jumped the hurdle and began sharing bits of my story with friends and family it became easier to write. I found peace as I wrote, but as I found the courage to share my experience I found an increased measure of peace. More peace followed as I let go of the guilt and stopped asking myself what more I could have done.

It will be rough for a long time. You need friends who will support you when times are so difficult that you can't help yourself. Have courage knowing that it will get better as you keep moving forward.

You will face many challenges. Metaphorical walls of guilt and loneliness will pop up when you least expect it, and you will need a boost to get over them. Find a buddy right away and work out a system of notifying them when you are stuck and need their assistance. You shouldn't grieve alone and you can't progress without help from someone who cares about you.

Thoughts and Impressions

Chapter 12
The Tragedy Is Not Yours to Keep

The year following David's death passed painfully. Halloween was less satisfying and felt more like trick than treat. Thanksgiving took on a literal meaning and caused each of us to reflect on true appreciation. It also caused us to grieve deeply over our loss. During the Christmas season we couldn't help but consider David when buying gifts. I even bought my wife a wireless speaker that resembled a Rubik's Cube in memory of her puzzle-loving brother. The gift would have been for him had he been present to accept it.

Halloween was only five days after David's death. We had spent a lot of time constructing a Groot costume for my oldest son. As much fun as it was building this thing out of foam noodles and twigs, it was difficult to celebrate our accomplishment because it seemed so pointless now. Regardless, we purchased a Rocket raccoon costume for my youngest son to accompany his brother.

They had worn their costumes just a few days prior at a neighborhood Halloween party and they had been looking forward to wearing them again for trick-or-treating. Now everything was different. Walking around the neighborhood asking for free candy seemed so frivolous, but for the sake of our young children we followed through. My wife and I mustered up the courage to face our friends and neighbors who would most certainly ask how we were doing. We were still very tender and would have rather crawled into a hole to avoid the inevitable question.

Needless to say, we were not in the mood to walk around the neighborhood and pretend to our friends and neighbors that we were okay. And we were not going to burden our friends with our true feelings. Regardless, we headed my mentor's advice and followed a normal routine, but most importantly, we mustered enough courage to allow our vulnerable hearts to go public.

Wouldn't you know it, we had the best weather we've ever had for trick-or-treating. We walked farther than we had ever before and knocked on nearly every door in our neighborhood. I saw homes that I hadn't seen before and met neighbors I hadn't before. These people had no idea what we had just gone through and treated us normally. Our courage to step outside provided opportunities for healing.

I remember allowing my mind to imagine that David was following us. Every shadow or unexplained sound, in my mind, was David reaching out to us from the grave. Aside from the fact that David really wasn't with us, we probably had the best Halloween ever, and I believe it was because we had the courage to allow ourselves to have fun and not feel guilty for it.

January provided an outlet for us to forget our sorrows a tiny bit. My wife planned a trip to San Diego with a stop in Anaheim first, and followed up with a trip to Universal Studios and SeaWorld. We spent the last few weeks of the year catching up at work in preparation for this needed vacation.

We spent Christmas at Katy's parent's house according to tradition, and especially out of necessity due to the circumstances. My parents and siblings spent New Year's Eve at my house and after the festivities my parents stayed the night.

New Year's Eve my father coughed all day but thought it was due to a lingering cold. Later in the evening, after everybody had gone to bed, he experienced chest pain and difficulty breathing, so my mother rushed him to the hospital.

I discovered them missing when I woke up in the morning and saw that their car was gone. I got a hold of my mother on her cell phone and learned that she had taken my dad to the hospital in the middle of the night, and they were still there running tests on his heart.

My wife and I packed up the kids and things to occupy their attention and rushed over to the hospital to see my dad. By the time we arrived, the doctor had determined my father's condition. He was diagnosed with congestive heart failure.

He spent the first week of January in the hospital, but I was only able to spend a few days with him before we left on vacation. I felt so guilty for leaving him and was very worried about his status. My mother called me while I was in California to inform me that my dad was released from the hospital and doing better. Still, the weather in southern California mirrored my feelings, gray and gloomy.

The weather in the west desert of northern Utah wasn't any different. The landscape that was usually white from salt was now covered in freshly fallen snow. It was bitterly cold and dry from Wendover, Nevada into Utah.

My family had just arrived home from our vacation in California when I received a call from my dad. His bad news was like a punch in the face. He informed me that his dad and brother were in a car accident just outside of West Wendover and were taken to the hospital in Murray, Utah.

I didn't even unpack, I just rushed to the hospital to see them. When I got there I was able to discern from my uncle that the roads were clear but the hour was long. Apparently they were coming home from a weekend trip to Wendover, Nevada and my grandfather was driving. He fell asleep at the wheel momentarily and overcorrected, sending his white hybrid careening off-road, flipping end over end until it finally rested on all four tires.

The trauma of that accident caused bleeding in Grandpa's brain. He spent the next four months in and out of hospitals; recovering for a few weeks in nursing homes only to be flown again to the hospital for more surgery to relieve pressure on his brain.

My uncle experienced that whole tragic accident with his father and was debilitated by similar head trauma. At this point my father had returned home to California and couldn't take any more time off work, so my family needed help and I was able to heed the call.

I was in the hospital with my grandpa every day for three months. While recovering in hospital after his second brain surgery, my uncle and I reviewed his living will that was explicit in not allowing resuscitative efforts. He made my uncle promise that he would let him die at home, so when we learned that Grandpa would not recover as we had hoped, we arranged hospice care in his home.

It was emotionally draining for me to watch the man I admired deteriorate to the point that he didn't even recognize me. It was also physically demanding trying to care for a grown man with the faculties of a child who just wanted to die.

The feeling that got me through the whole ordeal was that I had no regrets. It took courage to take time off work, even though work was extremely demanding and there was no guarantee I would have a job when I returned.

After Grandpa died, I returned to work. Thankfully, I had a job to return to, but I carried a heaviness in my heart. I remember speaking to friend at work one day about my experience and my concerns. She told me something profound, but so simple that I want to share it with you. She said that I would always have work, but I would never regret the time I spent with my grandfather.

We all know this is true, but how often do we practice what we preach? You may think that the work you are doing right now is the most important thing in the world, but really, it couldn't be less important when compared to giving time to someone you love.

This might sound contradictory to what I taught earlier about being consistent. In fact, it's quite in line with the concept of consistency as it relates to coping after the death of a loved one. Although I left my normal routine of work to take care of my grandfather, I returned to work immediately following his death. The truth is that it took a great amount of courage on my part to leave work for an extended amount of time in order to care for my grandfather. The fact that I had a job to return to was both remarkable and gratifying.

The underlying story, however, had an even more profound impact on me. It's unique and somewhat bizarre.

My grandfather lived fifteen minutes from my in-laws, so I stayed with them when I rested during the day after caring for Grandpa all night. I spent twelve to fourteen hours with Grandpa through the night with my cousin, and would return to my in-laws to sleep and relax during the daytime hours. Throughout my stay, I slept in David's vacant room.

I thought that staying in David's room would have been creepy or in some way disrespectful, but instead I felt very close him. I felt his pain through my own tears as I struggled with the emotional roller coaster that at this point seemed perpetual.

That short time I spent with my in-laws, coming home and relaxing with them every day, was very therapeutic for all of us. In order for me to stay in his room, my mother-in-law needed to clean and organize it, which was a big stumbling block. It required great courage on her part to move things and throw things away. Furthermore, allowing somebody to stay in his room must have required even more courage than I could understand.

Accepting the invitation to stay in David's room was initially difficult for me, but at the end of my stay it required even more courage to leave. I had become quite comfortable. Not to say that I had become comfortable with sadness and tragedy; merely I had become acquainted with mortality and had come to appreciate life. I also bonded more deeply with my in-laws.

One might have thought that with so much tragedy in such a short time I should have been a total wreck. I remember reasoning with myself at one point that I needed to keep calm and not play the victim. All this tragedy that surrounded me was not mine to keep. I was just a witness to the sorrow and a companion to the grief.

It's vital at these moments in your life that you don't internalize and hold on to grief. I didn't know how to do that at first so I experimented with a tactic used in business to drill down to the root cause of a problem. I first asked myself why I was so sad. As I searched for a reason, I discovered that there were several layers to my sadness. I continued to drill down through each layer until I came to the underlying cause of my sadness. I was able to focus all my attention on resolving the true cause of my sadness, which was much simpler and more effective than patching up superficial wounds.

The underlying cause of my sadness, and I expect it's true for most people, was the loss of opportunities. Regarding David, I would never see him graduate college or get married. I would never see a niece or a nephew from him. I would miss him at family reunions and Christmas parties. I would miss his smile and his laugh and his warm hugs. The list was endless.

To start the process of releasing grief, I first began reminding myself of opportunities achieved. I had to tell myself that what I counted as opportunities lost never existed, so I couldn't waste time grieving over fantasy. Instead, I appreciated the time I had with David.

Something good came from my loss. I began appreciating time with family as a profitable commodity. I placed value on memories made as a family and I found that it was much easier to let go of my sadness when new happy memories took root. I courageously removed the cloak of grief and guilt that weighed me down like sackcloth, and dispelled the disillusion that I needed to carry it around in order for others to appreciate my sorrow. After all, it wasn't mine alone to keep, and it was intolerant of me to think that I was the only one to have ever grieved.

- COMFORT -

Chapter 13
Comforting Memories Can Help You Heal

We all find comfort in various ways. Some people find comfort in keeping things, while others find it by giving things away. This section will discuss various ways in which I have found comfort. The next three chapters will illustrate several different coping strategies, from holding onto personal items and memories to giving the gift of life through tissue donation.

My son's room is adorned with Rubik's cube puzzles and Legend of Zelda memorabilia. These things don't appear out of place in a young boy's room and they don't stand out as heirlooms either, but they carry an emotional charge that chokes him up every time he holds them.

My brother-in-law, David loved to solve puzzles. Even greater was his fascination with video games. His room was full of both. He was most famous for the various shapes and sizes of Rubik's cubes that he could solve. His room was littered with various-sized, multi-colored, twisting puzzles. He was also a huge fan of the video game Legend of Zelda. He had enough memorabilia to stock a modest Comic Con booth.

My oldest son showed interest in playing with Rubik's Cubes previously, but after David was gone his interest evolved into obsession. He wanted nothing more than to hold one of David's cubes. He thought he wanted to solve one of the puzzle cubes, but soon realized that changing it from where David had left it was somehow sacrilegious. It was a treasure that brought him comfort when he needed to feel close to his uncle.

For the first few months following David's death, we all carried around small trinkets from his room. It made us feel close to him even though he was gone. There was nothing magical about the items, but each thing meant something to the person who carried it. It was infused with a memory that brought individual comfort.

I remember watching as friends and family visited my in-laws' home, and my mother-in-law allowed some people to take mementos from David's room. She understood that personal items brought comfort to those who loved David.

Christmas followed his death by a few months and his birthday followed Christmas by a few weeks. Although the pain of his absence was noted, we did a few things that helped us cope. First of all, when we saw something that reminded us of David, we bought it in his memory and gave it to somebody else who would appreciate it as much as he would have. Secondly, we celebrated the holiday as usual and remembered his birthday with a small celebration in his honor. Most importantly, my mother-in-law continued her tradition of setting up his Christmas tree alongside the others.

Friends and neighbors could always count on my mother-in-law to decorate her home with several Christmas trees. The largest went in the front room and was primarily for hanging her ornaments. Several more adorned the large window of the formal dining area, one for each of the kids. Friends visited and called it her personal festival of trees. She also had an annual tradition of purchasing Hallmark's ornaments for everyone in the family. The year of David's death was no different, and he got a new ornament along with everyone else.

Although she didn't adorn his tree with all of his ornaments, she carefully placed the ones that had special meaning to her. She said the process was therapeutic.

It's important to find comfort in the smallest thing. Some people might tell you to throw out everything that reminds you of your lost loved one because it hurts too much to see it. This kind of tactic might work for you. On the other end of the spectrum, I've seen some people develop unhealthy attachments to garbage because it was once touched by someone they loved and lost.

An important process at the medical examiner's office is inventorying personal effects of deceased individuals in order to return every last item to the family. We document and secure everything, including jewelry, coins, and even candy wrappers. It is not our duty to determine worth or assume worthlessness of anything. I've heard stories that some people find value and comfort in keeping the most unthinkable items, like candy wrappers. Comforting memories help you heal.

For example, my wife carried small trinkets of David's in her backpack while she ran the Spartan race. She said that carrying those items encouraged her and gave her strength, as if he was running beside her.

Another example is a humble painting that hangs on the wall in my family room. It portrays a single Samurai warrior saddled atop a light brown stallion amidst luscious emerald fields. It's roughly 16 X 20 inches and framed in a very modest gold painted frame. It wouldn't fetch top dollar at the Antique Roadshow, but to me the painting is priceless. It was painted by my grandmother, who died when I was seven. As her image begins to fade in my mind, all I need to do is look at the painting and my memory of her is revitalized.

Take a look around your home. What treasures capture your heart? Is it an old photograph of Grandma and Grandpa, or is it the antique frame that cradles it? Perhaps it's a crystal vase you inherited from your favorite aunt. These things might very well end up on the shelf of a local thrift store long after you're gone, but to you right now they have intrinsic value that money can't buy. Our homes are filled with such treasures. They are portals to our past and sometimes that can bring us comfort.

Chapter 14
Tissue Donation Brought Comfort to My Family

Although holding onto mementos can be comforting, giving can be just as healing. My father-in-law found comfort in donating much of his son's unused diabetic equipment and supplies to others in need. He valued the good that David's things could bring to other people.

Helping others was a big part of David's life. His love for others was real. I was always impressed by his generosity. He was known to walk the aisles of Walmart in his small town and watch for people who might be in need, especially around the holidays. After his death I learned that he once gave his entire paycheck to a family, knowing that his contribution would help the parents buy Christmas presents for their children. I only know this because one of the young daughters wrote a letter to David that we found while cleaning his room. The letter thanked him for making her family's Christmas unforgettable. That letter is among some of our family's treasured memories of David.

Another gift that is difficult to consider for some people is donating tissue, but urgency is critical when the time comes to make that decision. Tissue donation can be a sensitive subject for some people to discuss. In my work I've seen how valuable donation can be and the peace that can come from making the decision to donate. I have also witnessed families torn apart as they've tried to decide what would be best. Unknown to many is the fact that even though you make a decision to be an organ donor, your surviving next-of-kin still have to give authorization on your behalf. You can see where problems might arise between conflicting opinions amongst family members after you're dead if you haven't expressed your will to your family beforehand.

While my wife prepared to drive down and support her family on that dreadful October morning, she knew there were difficult questions that she would have to ask her grief-stricken parents. The first would be if they would consider donation. The knowledge she had that David was a giving and generous man in life supported the thought that he could continue that tradition even in the wake of tragic loss.

David's parents knew that donating parts of his body to others in need was the right thing to do. They worried, though, that the length of time before anyone found David had prevented donation. When my wife arrived to comfort her family she was able to address their concerns about tissue donation. Time was of the essence, and with some quick calls to my office and to Intermountain Donor Services their desire to help others became a reality.

Calls were made, permission was granted, and a recovery team was sent down right away. My father-in-law was overwhelmed with relief knowing that others could be granted a better life with David's gift. Both of his parents were able to find some peace and brightness in an otherwise dark and depressing day. David's death would not be a complete loss.

So even in death David was able to benefit numerous people. I dare say that tissue donation was probably one of the most comforting choices for his parents as they were bombarded with so many other overwhelming decisions to make so suddenly. They gained comfort in knowing that others' lives would be improved by their son's sacrifice.

It's really easy to simplify and divide people into two groups: haves and have-nots. Those who have stuff give some of their stuff to those who need it. However, it's much more than that. As illustrated above, the gift of life requires the ultimate sacrifice of one and is carried out by the culminating decision of many. The recipient also has a major role to play because of the magnitude of such a gift. Giving is such an important part of being human and is most successful when a connection is made.

Just the other day I was walking downtown with my wife and we were approached by an hysterical young man. Actually, he spotted us from quite a distance and came running toward us as we waited for a walking signal to cross the street. I almost leapt into the street without waiting for the signal just to avoid interacting with the man.

I made up all kinds of assumptions about the young man as he frantically relayed his situation. I also made up all kinds of assumptions about myself as I considered my response to his request for money. Clearly we were dealing with a "have-not" who spotted what he thought were a couple of "haves" so he thought he'd scam a few bucks.

As we continued to walk with him and allowed him to explain his situation my assumptions didn't matter anymore. He was not afraid to reveal his frailties, and in the process and unbeknownst to me, we were making a connection. My wife scrounged what she could from her purse and handed it to the man. He was extremely grateful for what little we offered and he hugged me as tears welled up in his eyes.

Later, after we had parted ways, I thought about how difficult it was for me to offer a few bucks from my nearly empty wallet, but how much more difficult it must have been for him to beg for money. I suddenly felt embarrassed about not having more to offer. His genuine gratitude for what little we gave comforted my wife. I realized at that moment that it wasn't about the money but rather something deeper and less tangible.

I don't know if that young man really needed money or if he was just trying to scam me for a few bucks; regardless, the end product from that momentary interaction was priceless. That end product that I'm talking about was a genuine connection to another human being.

As difficult as it might feel to be around other people while you mourn, and as much as you'd rather suffer alone, I assure you that connecting with people will bring you comfort. It's more than just giving of yourself or giving of your substance, it's about making a visceral connection while in such a vulnerable state.

After her brother's death my wife struggled with talking to people. She wasn't sure how to answer their questions. She really didn't want to talk about how she was feeling because she knew she wasn't doing well, but she also didn't want to burden her friends with her sorrow. In passing one day, a friend told her that it doesn't get any easier to cope with the death of a brother, regardless of how his life was taken. A natural disease claimed this friend's brother several years ago. My wife later told me that she was grateful for her friend's well-timed comment. It didn't require any explanation or further discussion and she found comfort.

It was simple, it didn't require her to talk about how she was feeling, and it connected the two of them more deeply. My wife said that she suddenly didn't feel alone in her struggle. It reminded her that everybody suffered the loss of loved ones. She found comfort in a shared a connection.

I'd like to reiterate that the end product of a genuine gift is the heartfelt bond between the giver and the receiver. Whether the gift is as magnanimous as organ donation or as simple as a well-timed comment, when given with real intent, both are blessed with comfort.

Chapter 15
Ghost Ticket to Disneyland

My wife, Katy, and I met while attending a community college in Price, Utah. The community college campus was only a few blocks away from her home. At the time she had three younger siblings, all under the age of seven. We took them everywhere with us. David, being the oldest of the three siblings, accompanied us on many occasions. He quickly became the most popular youngster on College of Eastern Utah campus.

Katy and I had a unique courtship. She was a Head Start teacher and we spent many dates creating learning activities for her students, which constituted drawing, coloring, and cutting paper. David helped with many of the projects. We spent much of our courtship surrounded by children, which I felt was a good introduction into parenthood. I treated David like a pseudo-son. When Katy and I took the little ones out with us on dates it felt like we were taking our "practice family" out on a test drive. We had a lot of fun.

That was fifteen years ago, and we could not have imagined what trials lurked around the corner of time. We were young and invincible 20-something-year-olds with the whole wide world in front of us.

We were married for five years when the whole family went to Disneyland to celebrate its 50th anniversary. David was twelve years old and full of life on that trip to the Magic Kingdom.

Ten years later we were back at Disneyland, only we were missing David on this trip. Mr. Disney established a place where people could go to imagine and have fun. It's considered to be the happiest place on Earth. But for those of us traveling with ghosts it was troubling.

August 2016 marked our family's return to Walt Disney's, "Happiest Place on Earth." The whole family was excited about this trip to our favorite theme park. We were back to celebrate the 60th anniversary, my mother-in-law's 60th birthday, and our little sister's 20th birthday. It promised to be an exciting and eventful week, yet everyone's hearts were heavy. We would be without David.

David loved Disneyland and collected Donald Duck memorabilia, which he proudly displayed throughout his bedroom. None of us suspected the emotional challenge it would be to return after ten years without one of our own.

We had purchased 5-day Park Hopper passes, which included one early entry per person. Each morning the family eagerly attempted to arrive early so that we could enjoy the park during the quieter morning hours. Each morning we struggled to arrive any earlier than regular park hours. On the fourth day, a group of us finally achieved getting ready early; however, we still had to make the mile-long trek into the park. If we walked we would not make it yet again. A decision was made that we would pile into the van, drop off the group at the front entrance, and the driver would park the car back at the hotel and make the trek back alone. I volunteered to be the driver. Everyone's excitement was high as I pulled up into the drop-off area and let everyone out.

Richard, Katy's youngest brother, was so excited that he had pulled out his park pass and was showing it off to everyone. The group exited and hurried towards the security bag check. I drove away to park the van.

What happened next is nothing short of amazing, and one of those little moments that helped remind us that David might be closer than we imagined.

Katy and the kids raced to get in line at the entrance, but our youngest pulled her back. Grandpa and Richard were not keeping up. She turned back to ask what the holdup was. Richard's ticket had vanished. It was in his hand one moment, gone the next. They checked the security bag tables, the ground, everywhere they had just been. They retraced steps, but the ticket had simply vanished.

Katy recalled that the lost ticket could be reprinted as long as its number could be identified. Our tickets had been purchased in two separate groupings. I received the desperate call to send a photograph of my ticket number so that Richard's ticket number could be discovered through the process of elimination. Those who had stayed behind to sleep were woken up to send pictures of their tickets as well. One by one the process of elimination began.

The ticket clerk discovered a snag. Her computer indicated that 5 tickets had been assigned to my family, and 5 tickets had been assigned to my in-laws.

"That can't be," my wife argued.

My wife purchased all of the tickets and had receipts for 9 tickets. My in-laws only had 4 tickets, but the clerk explained that all tickets were assigned in sequential order. The clerk also explained that it's the resort's policy to issue an individual number to each park-hopper pass and that those numbers are valuable and not handed out lightly.

The first set of five ticket numbers were all accounted for in my family. What was surprising was that the beginning number from my set and the two end numbers from my in-laws' set were identified, however there were two separate tickets in the middle of the sequence that were still not identified. If Richard's ticket was one of them, then who belonged to the other ticket?

Eventually they were able to identify that one of the numbers assigned to us had in fact been used, while the second had not. The clerk used the identified ticket number to issue Richard a replacement ticket and he was able to enter the park. The fact that we were issued an extra ticket, but not charged for it, remains a mystery.

The missing ticket was a small sign to us that David was there in spirit. He was not able to physically attend with us to celebrate and revel in the happiness, yet he was there. We all felt that if Richard had not lost his ticket we would never have known about the extra one. A stressful situation turned out to be one of the highlights of our trip. It was a little sign that we could keep moving forward after such loss and heartache.

Although our trip to Disneyland was fun and exciting, everything reminded us of our dearly departed brother Dave. There is in fact a tombstone at the Haunted Mansion with the inscription, "Dearly departed brother Dave." There was no escaping David at Disneyland. The nostalgia of remembering happy times accompanied by the sadness of lost opportunities was bittersweet.

As I watched the happy little children run and play all around me in the park I was reminded of when I first met David. He was an excitable, energetic 7-year-old with stars in his eyes. He could have ruled the world with his smile, but all that was gone now. Comfort did come though, but not all at once or when I wanted it to come. It came gradually and with time.

Every day we spent at the "happiest place on Earth" became brighter and brighter until eventually new memories took the place of sad ones and gratitude replaced regret. I began remembering David with a thankful heart instead of a broken one.

Visiting places that were special to you and your loved one can be comforting. However, be cautious that you are prepared for the tidal wave of emotions that will overwhelm you on your journey. It is important to note that you are not sitting at home stewing in your regrets, but rather out of the house and moving. There's nothing more damning than to be cooped up in sorrow.

- COMMUNICATION -

Chapter 16
Communication Is Key

Realizing that we all communicate through our emotions differently, I've come to the conclusion that we also grieve differently. One such realization came on the last day of our family trip to Disneyland. That last day was a long, tiring day and we wanted to take in as much as possible. None of us truly wanted to leave, but we knew we had a long drive home ahead of us.

It was about two hours until closing time and we were still gathering the troops. The infamous Disneyland Light Parade was underway and the sidewalks were littered with bodies. I couldn't breathe and I began tripping over people. I ducked into the first building that was open along Main Street and found a quiet hallway tucked behind a hat shop where we literally crashed.

Half of our group sprawled out in the lonesome hallway while the other half were in hot pursuit, attempting to wend their way through the massive hoard. I could still hear the music from the parade, but it was muffled, like hearing a marching band play from the inside of a parked car.

One of my kids asked what we were doing and my wife told them that we were getting ready to leave. My sister-in-law broke down when she heard that it was time to go. I assumed that she was upset because we were leaving sooner then she wanted. I made a lot of assumptions in that moment based on the emotion she was communicating and the timing. Little did I know her breakdown had nothing to do with leaving early?

We allowed for her to cry awhile before we finally peeled ourselves off of the carpeted floor in that solemn and memorable hallway. She expressed later that the thought of leaving the memories of David behind at Disneyland made her feel like she was losing him all over again.

I discovered at that moment that I sucked at reading minds. I wasn't very good at reading nonverbal communication either. I thought I knew what it meant to be empathetic, but I learned that night that I was doing it all wrong. I had made assumptions about how my sister-in-law was feeling, but I learned otherwise when she actually told me what she was feeling. The key was good old-fashioned verbal communication.

A different example of making a connection through good old-fashioned communication came a few years earlier when my wife and I decided to digitally scan old family photo slides as a birthday gift for her mother. We contacted her grandfather, who was the keeper of the slides, and set date to visit him. You need to understand that at this stage in our marriage I barely knew her grandfather. We had developed a decent relationship over the course of family events and drop-by visits and I had developed my assumptions about him through those interactions.

We purchased a digital slide scanner and carved out a few days in our schedule. We had a few months to get it done, but we had no idea how long it was really going to take. The first day was spent visiting and building a relationship of trust. I hadn't fully appreciated the complexity of the project I had started until day two. I learned that it wasn't just about collecting and gathering all the boxes of slides and scanning them one by one. It was much more.

Each of the 4000 slides was like a key that unlocked priceless memories. My only regret later on was that I didn't record our conversations. Our "simple" project of scanning old pictures turned into four separate weekend trips and almost 100 hours of processing.

What I got from those trips to Idaho Falls to see Grandpa wasn't just the conversion of family photos in a more convenient format. It was the conversion of assumptions into understanding by talking to each other. We made a connection during the time we spent together.

Before this time the assumptions I made about my wife's grandfather were based on stories told to me by other family members and the circumstances I found him in when we first met.

He was a retired lieutenant colonel from the United States Air Force. He flew C-class airplanes during his time in the military. Afterwards he became a high school science teacher. He was divorced from my wife's grandmother and married to a much younger woman. He was very well spoken and highly intelligent. He seemed to know everything about anything.

I felt incredibly out of place around him, so I decided to play the part of a student and that helped a little. All the while I worked off the image I created of him based on the stories I was told. Everything changed thanks to the long hours reminiscing over old family photographs and watching his eyes glisten as he talked about his family.

Afterwards my wife commented that she was surprised that he allowed me to handle the slides and even scan them. She said that she had always known him to be carefully guarded and protective of the family photos.

We both came away from that experience changed men. He opened up and shared a part of himself. I learned that you can't judge a man by his rank and especially not by his mistakes.

When I was asked to speak at his funeral I had no problem commemorating this family patriarch with heartfelt, genuine, loving words. During our time together he taught me a principle that I would like to share with you as I close this chapter.

He said, "Never forget the defining moments in your life. They almost always involve family. Some are good and some are bad, but…" he paused and then with a quiver in his voice he said, "it's important to forgive quickly and never stop loving."

I want to add, "never stop communicating." With proper communication, assumptions are stopped dead in their tracks, misunderstandings can be forgiven quickly, and your capacity to love is quickened.

Chapter 17
Feeling Unworthy To Grieve

It was Saturday and the sun was shining. I found a lot of outdoor tasks to fill my time. It had been cold for so long that the warmth of the sun felt invigorating. Working outdoors with my hands has always calmed my mind. Remembering that one of my strategies for coping was consistency I poopy scooped - a chore that could have easily been done by my boys. Somehow, today, I felt that I just needed to do it.

It really was a beautiful day and I felt so accomplished afterward that I decided to reward myself with a little rest and relaxation. I completely pushed this book out of my mind and sat down in my recliner to relax for the afternoon. My stereo blasted Michael Jackson from the living room and I was loving it.

Next, Stevie Wonder came on the radio singing "Superstition." He didn't even get the first line out when the station abruptly changed to Paul Cardall playing "Gracie's Theme." Now, if you've ever heard this haunting melody you'll know exactly how I felt at that moment. If you've never heard it, I encourage you to listen to it while you read this chapter.

Music opens your heart and your mind to communication. My heart was certainly opened at that moment. A wave of emotions washed over me which started in my toes and filled me until it came gushing out my eye sockets. I listened to every inspirational note as the music provoked repressed thoughts.

The music ended as abruptly as it began, and Stevie Wonder finished "Superstition." Talk about spooky, but that's how I operate. After all, I work in a morgue for a living. I ran to my computer, emboldened to offer you something inspiring, and that's what I intend to do as we continue discussing how communication will help you cope with the death of a loved one.

I thought about how forgiveness was a healthy consequence of communication. And then it hit me, I hadn't considered that sometimes the person you need to forgive is yourself. In order for that to happen, you need a broken heart. I'm not talking about the kind of broken that is usually held together by a wall that you build around it for protection. A walled-up heart will not allow forgiveness. I'm talking about the kind of broken heart that opens up like a plastic Easter egg and allows you to fill it with yummy things.

I've had the good fortune of meeting Mr. Cardall and listening to his music in person. It's even more heart wrenching live. I was humbled and inspired by his music and his story. It speaks of hope and gratitude. When I hear his music I'm taken to a place of love and redemption.

For me, music is the purest, most powerful form of communication. The right song will change my mood and open my heart. Forgiveness of others also requires a broken heart, but especially when the one you need to forgive is yourself.

Sometimes inspiration comes exactly when you need it and sometimes it comes as a happy accident. The key is to not brush it off when it comes. The left side of our brain searches for a logical explanation to situations like the abrupt music change that I experienced and tries to dismiss the happy accident as a coincidence. Luckily, the right side of my brain interpreted the shift in musical genre that day as a message.

Mr. Cardall's inspirational piano music spoke to my soul and prepared my heart to receive forgiveness. I certainly needed it in order to move past my impediment and finish my story.

I had been feeling guilty since my brother-in-law's death, and that guilt was holding me back for two reasons. Reason number one generated from the shoulda-coulda-woulda game that I had played out in my mind that I should have seen it coming and could have saved him had I intervened. Reason number two was the guilt for being so sad and not feeling worthy of owning that grief. It seemed to me that if anybody was worthy of holding on to that grief more than me it would have been his parents. Contrarily, I saw his mother and father coping well, and there I was crying every time someone mentioned his name.

This is where communication saved me. I took the opportunity when we were together on one occasion and asked my mother and father-in-law how they were doing. I expressed how I was not coping well and I felt like I wasn't worthy to be grieving so deeply. They both sat on my living room couch as I sat across from them on the floor. Everyone else had left the room so we were alone to speak freely.

I remember being so nervous to bring up the topic. I considered, "What if their healing hearts were still tender and I reopened their wounds too early by talking about it?"

We started talking about this book I was writing as a way of coping with my own grief. I told my mother-in-law that I was writing it for her and every other mother in her same place. We discussed the lack of resources in their rural community and how they had hosted a group therapy night under the auspice of helping their friends who also lost children to suicide.

I commended them for their valiant efforts and asked them how they were truly doing. Red, puffy eyes stared back at me as mine filled with tears. With cracked voices they expressed their daily struggles. I suddenly felt safe sharing mine. My guilt vanished as I told them my struggle with feeling unworthy to grieve for the loss of their son.

We didn't move from our places in the living room, but I felt their loving and accepting arms around me as we shared our feelings in that safe environment. We discovered several things as we continued visiting that we will forever hold sacred in our hearts. Needless to say, communicating our feelings openly in the safety and security of my home with true love and acceptance disbanded the guilt that had held me hostage previously.

I invite you to create a safe environment to share what you are going through. It can be in the safety and comfort of your home or the solitude of your vehicle. It doesn't even need to be to a real person. Some people have found success talking to an imaginary person.

The key is that you speak aloud the feelings that are keeping you down. Whether the person you talk to is real or imaginary, you must first ask their permission to speak freely. If they are real, then asking permission creates a safe environment for rewarding communication. If the person is not real, then it creates a space that feels less ethereal and allows for advantageous communication. In any case, it is important for you to open up in order to release any negative emotions that are weighing you down.

Chapter 18
Peer Helpers

There are many forms of communication. Any method could be critical to your healing. It's important to understand them and find the one that works for you.

I want to take you back now over twenty years to when I was in junior high school. As a ninth grader I had the option of joining certain clubs. The school counselor invited me to join a special club that changed my life forever. The skills I developed while participating in this club were provident.

The group was called Peer Helpers and our job was to listen to our peers. Our goal was to give our friends a safe forum to destress. There was a pivotal moment as a peer counselor that was a real game changer for me. I might have been a different person minus that turning point. I truly believe that every decision I've made in my life has been a ripple effect from that one choice.

By helping my peers, I learned a lot about myself. Being a Peer Helper empowered a change that helped me discover my worth and define my purpose.

Halfway through the school year our group had an opportunity to travel two hours north on a field trip to Salt Lake City. The Salt Palace Convention Center hosted a series of seminars and professional workshops for peer counseling groups. This trip was the first time I had ever traveled to the big city without my parents. I felt adventurous staying in a hotel without them.

The Salt Palace was huge and foreign. It was scary and exciting all at the same time. There were more people at that convention center than in my whole town. I even remember seeing a television news reporter walk past and thinking I had made it big time to be in the same place as somebody I recognized from TV. To this day, when I see her reporting the news I'm taken back to the nostalgia of that moment.

The day was spent attending lectures that talked about confidentiality and trust. I remember attending workshops that demonstrated how to actively listen by having us practice with partners and repeat back to them to clarify what they had said.

At the end of the day our counselor rounded us up and assembled us in one of the rooms. I assumed we were going to talk about dinner plans, but I was wrong.

I should have known by the serious look in her eyes. It was the same look I had seen many times before, glaring back at me when my parents had something important to say. It wasn't stern, but it was very concerned, with an edge of fear. She drew in a deep breath and then laid it on us.

We learned that one of our classmates had died by suicide while we were away. For me he was more than a classmate, he was my buddy. It took me a long time to forgive myself. My heart was encrusted with the facts, and the fact was that I was hundreds of miles from home learning how to help my friends cope with disappointment and heartache, and my friend was home needing me more than ever and I wasn't there for him.

I felt helpless. I mean helpless to the point that I began to question my own existence. I wondered if there was a point to any of it. I doubted my convictions and whether or not I had a purpose. A dark cloud settled over my life for the duration of the school year. Honestly, I don't think any of us fully recovered from that experience, but we kept moving forward. That was about all we could do for a long time.

Immediately following the tragedy, his family did the most gracious thing imaginable. They opened their home for friends and family to gather and talk through their individual pain and grief. I will never forget finding my way to a darkened corner of the family room and watching as the room filled with classmates and neighbors.

I had no idea what I would talk about. I hoped that somehow, by the grace of God, my being there would miraculously heal my wounded soul. After about an hour of going around the room listening to story after story about this great young man who would never get married or have children of his own I realized that I wasn't getting better. In fact, I was feeling worse.

Finally, I reflected on some of the things I learned at the conference in Salt Lake City. I realized that by taking a passive role in this group therapy-type experience I wasn't going to gain anything. When it was my turn to talk again, instead of passing I decided to speak up.

I don't remember anything that was said that night. The stories that were shared all those years ago have all faded, but the feelings are ever present. I recollect that as I allowed myself to cry in front of people while sharing my thoughts and feelings, and as I watched everyone around me crying, something miraculous happened. We grew closer and stronger together.

I continued with Peer Helpers and transitioned into People Helping People in high school. I don't know if I ever really helped any of my classmates, but I owe a debt of gratitude to those organizations and my counsellors for saving me. I'm a better communicator because of them.

Opening our hearts and allowing others to witness our vulnerabilities actually makes us stronger. This is important so I'll say that again in a different way. As we communicate and allow ourselves to cry in public, our capacity to connect increases, thus increasing our ability to heal.

- CHARITY -

Chapter 19
A Meaning-Focused Coping Strategy Is Positive

It is argued that a meaning-focused coping strategy is positive. This technique requires a person to find meaning from tragedy, the so called "silver lining." How do you apply this concept when the tragedy you've experienced is the loss a loved one to death? You find something meaningful to focus on and then do something about it. You might carry out a dying wish or volunteer at a favorite charity. By combining your focus with social coping strategies such as support groups and charity work, you lose yourself. The benefit of losing yourself in the service of others is that you get your life back. You forget your pain and suffering, if even for a moment, while helping to ease the pain and suffering of those you serve.

I've found solace and personal satisfaction in years of research into suicide prevention. It has opened my eyes to the uncertainties about suicide behavior that have haunted me my whole life. I think that one of the worst feelings to harbor, that will eventually lead to despair, is uncertainty. I don't know about you, but for me, not knowing eats away at the lining of my stomach and gives me migraines. Needless to say, I hate surprises.

I recall feeling very ill a few years ago. This went on for quite a while, so after a lot of encouragement by my wife I made an appointment to see my primary care physician. I remember sitting in the tiny exam room on disposable white paper as he looked me over and performed a few routine physical tests. He needed me to provide samples to the lab for testing, so he instructed me on what to do and guided me down the hall to the lab. After I had supplied the required samples a nurse escorted me back to the tiny exam room and told me that the doctor would be back in to talk to me.

By the time the doctor returned I had already made up a half a dozen stories in my mind about what he was going to say. It still didn't prepare me for what he actually said. My doctor presented a differential diagnosis that was devastating but somehow satisfying. I couldn't believe it. I was just given terrible news, but I felt better for it. How was that possible?

The key was knowing. Suddenly the smothering fog of uncertainty was pushed out by answers from somebody who knew better. Even though the news was shocking, it provided me with a destination. I was no longer in the dark about my fate. My new direction put me in front of specialists who knew more than I and could help me refine my path and point me in helpful and healing directions.

Something miraculous happened. I started smiling again. My heart wasn't as heavy and my mind became more clear. Over the course of a few months of therapy and treatment I felt better than I had in a long time. I came away from that experience with a deeper appreciation for association and collaboration. As much as I liked to do things by myself, I realized that involving others who knew more or had more experience was vital to my success.

There are many organizations available in which you can participate, whether for yourself or for someone else. They offer fundraising activities for research and prevention along with health care treatment and awareness. There are groups that specialize in substance abuse, mental illness, and local bereavement support. There are also local victim's advocate groups that can be contacted through your local police department or sheriff's office. Every year Utah Department of Health provides a list to its employees regarding the myriad of charitable organizations to which they can choose to donate a percentage of their meager paychecks. I cannot list them all, however, I would like to mention two that I'm most familiar with.

First of all, there is National Alliance on Mental Illness (NAMI) whose mission is to build better lives for those affected by mental illness. I have had an opportunity to participate in their annual walk that focuses on raising money and awareness for treatment and recovery for people with mental illness. Second is the American Foundation for Suicide Prevention.

I'm affiliated with these organizations for two reasons. My initial purpose is personal, as I know many people who suffer with mental illness such as depression, bi-polar disorder, and substance abuse. Secondly, I'm associated with the University of Utah, Dept. of

Psychiatry, where I've been working with a team of researchers and doctors searching for understanding into suicide behavior. Participation in this research motivates me and helps me cope with the loss of friends and family to suicide.

A third example I know, and arguably one of the largest in the state for charity work, is known locally as The Festival of Trees. Most people begin planning for next year's festival the day after the current year's event ends. It's that rewarding! Everything displayed at the festival is donated and for sale. This includes elaborately decorated Christmas trees, door wreaths, gingerbread houses, and homemade crafts. The astounding part is that 100% of the proceeds are returned to Primary Children's Medical Center in Salt Lake City. The money provides medical treatment for children. Could there be any cause nobler than helping a child?

Chapter 20
American Foundation for Suicide Prevention

Just a month before my brother-in-law died by suicide, the whole family was together for an annual family reunion. One of our traditions was to go to the farmers market at Pioneer Park in Salt Lake City. As I wandered the park looking at all the cool artistic wares being sold at each of the many booths that zigzagged throughout the park, I happened upon one for American Foundation for Suicide Prevention. My professional interest in suicide prevention caused me to stop and talk to the volunteers.

We enjoyed a pleasant and productive conversation about current issues and recent publications into the understanding of suicide. I graciously accepted a business card and a few pamphlets about upcoming events. After carefully placing the business card in my wallet, we shook hands and parted ways. I had no way of knowing that I would need that business card for personal assistance in just a few short weeks.

I reflected on all the awareness campaigns and suicide prevention activities I attended as a professional and remembered soaking in everything on a purely academic level. The amount of support and the tremendous amount of good that came from each event touched my heart. This year I attended one such event, Out of the Darkness Walk, not as a healthcare professional, but as one who suffers. My family walked in memory of our beloved David.

As we approached the event and looked around for a place to park the van, I felt something more powerful than I had ever in previous years. Thousands of people gathered for the same purpose and today I was one of them. I was no longer a researcher looking in from the outside. My mind was overwhelmed and my heart was heavy to see so many families coming together in various levels of grief.

My mother-in-law invited friends who had recently lost their child to suicide and I could sense the wound was fresh. They showed an appreciable difference in their reaction to the event compared to my family, who were a few months ahead of them in healing. I saw fear and sadness in their expressions. It was the kind of fear that came from hopelessness and uncertainty. I felt a burden of helplessness because I could not comfort them.

When we had all gathered, we walked toward the registration area. Things became very real for me at the check-in booth, where we were encouraged to write David's name on a sticker badge that indicated who we were commemorating on our walk. In years past I read the names on others' badges in a clearly professional manner and my heart ached for the families. Now I was one of those families, and putting David's name on my sticker and placing it on my shirt felt like a hot branding iron on my aching heart.

After we had all stuck David's name on our shirts we had another choice to make. There were several piles of colored Mardi Gras beaded necklaces to choose and wear while we walked around the park. They were called Honor beads, and each color represented something about you. You could tell by the color of beaded necklace somebody was wearing whether they had lost a child to suicide or a sibling, or whether they were struggling personally.

I never considered the power contained in a simple color beaded necklace. But there they were, in all their rainbow splendor, mocking me. They held my secrets and they were going to tell the world. I wasn't entirely sure I was ready for others to know. I wrestled with the question, "Should I really pick all the colors that truthfully represented me?"

The choices were overwhelming. Orange Honor beads were for people who had lost a sibling to suicide. Was I worthy to wear an orange necklace? After all, David was my brother-in-law and not my biological sibling.

I stood at the booth for what felt like a lifetime just staring at the sign that accompanied the beaded necklaces. I thought about all the times I had eaten at one of my favorite restaurants and received a beaded Mardi Gras necklace with my order. The only thought I gave to that was picking my favorite color. Now all I could think of was how overwhelming picking these colors was going to be for me.

Finally, my wife slipped an orange necklace over my head. God bless her! I suddenly felt very heavy. I became almost as sad as the morning I received the news of David's death. I'm telling you it was heartbreaking to acknowledge it all over again. Thoughts of David came rushing through my mind and tears rolled down my cheek.

At that point I was ready to move on, I could have stopped with the orange beads, but something urged me to continue confessing. I owed it to myself to participate 100%. Suddenly I found myself reaching for and grabbing purple beads and green beads. More tears flowed as I straddled those necklaces around my neck. Emotions that I had kept very personal were now in the open. They weren't inside anymore, now I was wearing them like a scarlet letter for the world to see.

The real test of my emotions came when I looked over at my wife and daughter, who were standing next to me. They were obviously going through the same internal struggle. I noticed that they would pick up a strand and then put it back down only to pick it up again. Eventually, just like me, they had slipped on more than a few different colors themselves. I had no idea. We hugged and cried together, and even though that moment only lasted a few minutes, the impression it left on my heart and in my memory will last forever.

Whether you find comfort in connecting with others at large awareness campaigns or you find comfort in smaller groups, the concept is the same. Awareness and advocacy helps everyone involved. Participation provides funding for research and prevention. Most importantly, the participant finds comfort in connecting with others.

I urge you to participate. Find a local event and attend. You'll be grateful you did. Not only show up, but participate 100%. Doing so just might be the beginning of your roadmap to healing.

Chapter 21
Festival of Trees

Charity and gratitude can often be found together. My in-laws have a tradition of attending a local charity event every year. This event benefits patients at Primary Children's Hospital. David's many trips to the hospital, as well as several occasions for our own children, helped instill in us an appreciation for the quality services offered to young children and their families at Primary Children's.

Each year our family looks forward to the week after Thanksgiving when we attend the annual Festival of Trees. The Festival of Trees is a week-long fundraising event. The festival is held in a large exposition center. The center is filled with Christmas trees, gifts, a sweet shop, children's corner, Santa Claus, quilts, and more. It's a marvelous way to bring in the Christmas spirit. The displays, trees, treats, and handmade items are all donated and auctioned off throughout the week. 100% of the proceeds are donated to families in need at Primary Children's Hospital.

Families, friends, and church groups spend hundreds of hours building and decorating trees to donate. Each donor has the opportunity to write a story about their tree and the reason for donating. These trees are frequently donated in the honor of someone. My wife and mother-in-law take time to carefully read the stories and dedications. They often need a tissue at the ready as they read about time lost with loved ones. We marvel at the displays of gratitude in such extreme time of loss and heartache.

The dedications are filled with stories of families who are grieving over the loss of loved ones to accident, sickness, and genetics. There are no stories of anger. Many share their love and gratitude for the help and services that they received. These families are seeking to find a way to give back to the community, to help others.

The months that followed the loss of David were difficult. The family considered doing a tree, but our pain was so fresh we just couldn't manage it. Festival week came and went. The family determined that we wanted to do a tree in David's honor the following year. A theme was chosen, messages were sent out to family and friends, and the project began.

Over the coming year we found items that we knew David would have loved. Each item was purchased with the statement that this is for David. A quilt was commissioned, color schemes were followed. Everyone felt a connection to David as they gathered precious gifts and donated their time and talent in his honor.

I watched my young children find happiness again as they crafted ornaments for "David's tree." My mother-in-law would buy things "for David" and the calm she felt was visible. Everyone who played a part in preparing the tree experienced a healing that was unexpected. We began to understand more deeply the healing received by those who donate trees every year. The process brought peace. It helped us feel closer to our lost loved one. We felt happy knowing that our time and efforts would benefit others and perhaps give them a little more time with their loved one.

Not all stories at the Festival of Trees end tragically. Regardless, they are heart wrenching. Each tree is donated and accompanied by a heart-touching story. The stories express gratitude and love, hope and humility, and sometimes happy endings. It can be difficult for me to read the stories as I walk through the forest of brightly decorated trees. Each decoration represents the heart of an innocent child. Every stuffed animal and action figure tells a story. The stories that are familiar to me from work take on a personality as I read each thoughtfully crafted sentence on the back of the place card displayed in front of each Christmas tree. Emotions I suppressed earlier so I could survive work rush back with a vengeance when I read these stories of love and hope and tragedy.

However heart wrenching the moment might be, it is a good experience overall to see so many people come together to give hope and promise to others who have experienced similar tragedy. My annual walk through the Festival of Trees is therapeutic. It helps me process each situation by witnessing positive resolution to tragedy.

I encourage you to look for opportunities to help others. If you are the one needing help, then resolve to search it out. Allow others to help you. You may be surprised to find somebody who understands exactly what you're going through. You will find that by serving others you will forget yourself, and your own problems will become secondary or even forgotten all together.

- CONCLUSION & ENCOURAGEMENT -

Chapter 22
Finding a Coping Mechanism That Works For You

Twenty years ago I had a myriad of opportunities in front of me, but my eye was focused on a single purpose. I wanted to help people and I thought the best way to make the greatest difference was to work in medicine. It never crossed my impressionable mind that medical professionals were normal people susceptible to the same sorrows as everyone else.

Living beings cannot escape tragedy no matter whom they are or where they live. I witness atrocities every day from the youngest of us to the oldest, from the wealthiest to the most poor. As a medical examiner assistant I've accepted two realities: death is no respecter of persons, and someday, inevitably I would have to autopsy somebody I loved.

Over the past fifteen years I have miraculously and narrowly escaped the inevitable. Sometimes I was away on vacation when somebody I knew died and was autopsied by the medical examiner. In the case of my brother-in-law, a deputy medical examiner handled his examination remotely, so his body was never taken to the central office.

Although I missed the autopsies of loved ones, the pain of death still stung. I attended funerals and offered condolences to so many people that the pain began to dull. I remember attending my maternal grandfather's funeral and searching for any emotion. I found nothing.

I was sitting in a small viewing room watching friends and family pay their last respects to my dearly departed grand-dad. A friend approached me and said, "It's good to see you."

Without a second thought I responded, "I'm happy to be seen rather than viewed."

I saw his eyebrows crinkle up and the incredulous look in his eyes pierced the crusty coating around my heart.

We both glanced toward my grandpa's casket and back again. He put his arm on my shoulder and smiled. He knew I meant no disrespect, but he must have suspected that my emotions were buried very deep.

He sat with me for a while with his arm around my shoulders. We didn't say a word the entire time, but his sincerity spoke volumes in my mind. His closeness helped me feel safe. That moment marked the beginning a long journey of refinement. I could no longer hide behind my theories of dissociation or trite humor. I feared the worst. Had I become so callous that I lost the ability to show emotion? Dissociation seemed to me like a practical tool for dealing with death on a daily basis, but I feared it was whittling away my soul.

Tragedy began to strike closer and closer, like a rogue funnel cloud striking and then receding momentarily before striking again. It seemed like we hadn't fully recovered from the previous tragedy before another one happened when my wife's grandfather died. I couldn't run from these. I requested a lot of time off from work to deal with the stress of each tragedy head on. This led to more stress, since people at work found it necessary to remind me of how much time I was taking off.

Friends, I'm telling you, I was at the end of my rope and I wanted to let go. I was beginning to appreciate why some people preferred death. It wasn't something I had considered, but I saw a glimpse of how easy it would be to consider suicide as a solution. This idea frightened me. I felt like I was unraveling.

I continued to go to work day after day, hating every minute but pretending like I was living my dream. Everyday tested my strength. I felt like I was constantly putting out forest fires with a garden hose. I had a few trusted friends who would take me to lunch as often as time would permit so we could talk. We connected as we commiserated.

For a time I felt guilty for lying to myself and pretending to my employees that everything was fine. I secretly applied to several other jobs hoping that I could escape the torment. My credentials were flawless, but I couldn't seem to land the job. Well, folks, it's no wonder. I was miserable and it showed.

My biggest worry was about my family and the damage my bad attitude was doing to my innocent children, who were no doubt battling their own demons. I thought back to the comment I made to my friend at my grandfather's funeral and realized that I was glad to be alive. I asked myself how I could take for granted what I had.

I had an intelligent, loving, independent wife who supported me in everything. My children were well-adjusted and genuinely good. I had a job that was the envy of everyone I knew. So what was my problem and how was I going to fix it?

I had a professor in college who would say, "Write this down. This will be on the test." Friends, this is the part where you get out your pen or highlighter and start marking, if you haven't already.

My transformation began as an idea. It was a brief moment in time when I made a decision and that decision expanded into action. That moment sparked the idea for this book and has brought sunshine back into my soul.

The idea was simple. I realized that I had the power within me to make a change. I was happy before and I could be happy again. All I needed to do was to continue doing the things that had made me happy before. Easy, right?

Eventually I made the decision to crack the crusty shell that had found its place around my heart. That's when I finally saw things clearly. I began working backwards to figure out the puzzle to my success in order to share it with you. So let me recap.

The sections in this book were neither chronological nor additive. There are no established pathways to coping with death. The order doesn't matter as much as the practice of each of the seven techniques outlined in this book: 1. Consistency, 2. Choice, 3 & 4. Courage and Camaraderie, 5. Comfort, 6. Communication, 7. Charity.

> 1.   Consistency is a direct route to healing. Jumpstart your routine prior to your tragedy and become consistent in order to maintain a healthy body and mind. I'll never forget walking around my neighborhood trick-or-treating with my kids only four days after their uncle's suicide. It would have been so easy to justify sitting home with the lights out that Halloween. Walking around the neighborhood was uncomfortable at first but rewarding later.

> 2.   Making positive choices is an important step toward healing. I talked about the interview

questions I asked job candidates. The successful candidates accepted death as a natural part of life and chose to not let it affect their attitude. As a point of reference, my roadmap to healing began when I chose to write this book.

3 & 4.   Courage and camaraderie are vital components to healing. They keep you on the path, moving forward. Without courage to tackle tough obstacles and friends to help me over impassible walls I could not have finished a single Spartan race. Having courage to stand against the overwhelming trials in your life will allow you to defy all odds much like young shepherd, David, versus Goliath, the giant warrior of Gad. Having the support of friends will add a measurable level of success.

5.   You can find comfort in so many things. Find comfort in celebrating milestones and anniversaries; as painful as they will be, it's important to not ignore them. It's important to share them with others. My in-laws found comfort in tissue donation, knowing that others would benefit. My family found comfort in unexplained

superstitions that made it feel like our lost brother was still near.

6.   Communication can be a difficult coping technique for some people. It's easy to make assumptions, so much so that we often do it without thinking. Sometimes the truth hurts so much that we'd rather lie to ourselves than talk to somebody about our pain. Consider this. Sometimes communicating doesn't require any words at all. Crying on the shoulder of somebody you trust might be all the therapeutic communication you need today.

7.   Charity offers the greatest reward. Charity requires pure love without hope of anything in return. Although, miraculously, you will receive something in return. The reward is something wholesome and good that will fill the void in your broken heart and begin mending your saddened soul.

These seven coping strategies were successfully tested by my family. I encourage you to pattern these ideas and incorporate them into your life so that you will find the sunshine you so desperately seek.

Find your own coping mechanisms and report to me on your progress at LinksofCourage.com.

We're in this together!

Thoughts and Impressions

_____

_____

_____

_____

_____

_____

_____

_____

_____

_____

_____

_____

_____

_____

_____

_____

ABOUT THE AUTHOR

W. Brandon Callor was born in Price, Utah, where he lived most of his life. For a short period during his adolescence his family lived in San Francisco; although they moved after only a short time there, Brandon left his heart and yearns for each opportunity to return to the city by the bay. He now lives in Cottonwood Heights, Utah, where he enjoys hiking, running, and watching his three children grow up at the foot of Big Cottonwood Canyon. You will often find Brandon writing while his gorgeous wife reads over his shoulder, no matter how much he harasses her about not doing it.

Brandon would love to hear your story. Write to him at Brandon.Callor@linksofcourage.com and share your success.

160

Made in the USA
San Bernardino, CA
01 March 2020

64989759R00091